Tomorrow's Innovators

Tomorrow's Innovators

Essential Skills for a Changing World

Dennis Adams and Mary Hamm

ROWMAN & LITTLEFIELD EDUCATION
A division of
ROWMAN & LITTLEFIELD PUBLISHERS, INC.
Lanham • New York • Toronto • Plymouth, UK

KH

Published by Rowman & Littlefield Education
A division of Rowman & Littlefield Publishers, Inc.
A wholly owned subsidiary of The Rowman & Littlefield Publishing Group, Inc.
4501 Forbes Boulevard, Suite 200, Lanham, Maryland 20706
www.rowman.com

10 Thornbury Road, Plymouth PL6 7PP, United Kingdom

Copyright © 2013 by Dennis Adams and Mary Hamm

British Library Cataloguing in Publication Information Available

Library of Congress Cataloging-in-Publication Data

Adams, Dennis M.
Tomorrow's innovators : essential skills for a changing world / Dennis Adams and Mary Hamm.
p. cm.
ISBN 978-1-4758-0080-7 (cloth : alk. paper) -- ISBN 978-1-4758-0081-4 (pbk. : alk. paper) -- ISBN 978-1-4758-0082-1 (electronic)
1. Education--Curricula--Philosophy. 2. Creative teaching. 3. Education--Effect of technological innovations on. 4. Technological literacy--Study and teaching. 5. Information literacy--Study and teaching. I. Hamm, Mary. II. Title.
LB1570.A27 2012
375'.001--dc23
2012026704

The paper used in this publication meets the minimum requirements of American National Standard for Information Sciences Permanence of Paper for Printed Library Materials, ANSI/NISO Z39.48-1992.

Printed in the United States of America

11/12/13

Contents

Preface

This book focuses on approaches and methods for infusing twenty-first-century skills like creativity, innovation, and adaptability into basic subject matter lessons. It also explores the cognitive nature of learning, standards across the curriculum, and the pedagogical implications of technology. Along the way, we hope to provide educators with insights into current educational issues and possibilities for translating new ideas into practical classroom applications.

Essential skills for a changing world have a lot to do with problem solving, mastering basic subjects, creative thinking, technological innovation, and the ability to collaborate. Also, a key skill is the ability to quickly survey a wide range of sources and to synthesize what's important. Knowing what's worth paying attention to matters more than ever—especially when you consider the increasing flood of data engulfing us.

Broad technological, cultural, and educational trends are challenging old assumptions and inviting new dreams. Whether it is the challenges associated with globalization, new technology, or instructional reform, there is always a danger of change biting back. So, it is important to think about the costs, the benefits, and skills needed to do well in a connected and complicated world.

The cultural context young learners find themselves in has a lot to do with how they develop an understanding of the way the world works and the way they go about meeting daily challenges. Values, norms, and beliefs play key roles in the way a student approaches learning. Teachers can't do it alone. Schools and community-based support have to be wrapped around each other in a way that provides a good educational foundation.

We may not be able to guarantee every student a great home life, but working together, we should be able to provide them all with a good education. The key to the quality of learning in the classroom is the teacher. Having a good teacher is the biggest single determinant of how well students learn to navigate the unsettling realities found along the road to arrive at a deep understanding of whatever subject is being studied.

Unfortunately, much of the oxygen surrounding the schools debate has been consumed by such structural concerns as grading teachers, more tests, charter schools, and a longer school year. All of these are important issues. But what matters even more is developing and keeping quality teachers who can deal with the characteristics of effective instruction in the technology-intensive twenty-first century.

One of the most important trends unfolding in the world today involves the widespread distribution of tools of communication and innovation. Information comes to us on paper and increasingly through the powerful images and sounds of electronic media. Preparing students for the digitized and connected world of today requires major changes in our thinking. To be successful in such an environment requires updating schools in a way that breathes new life into teaching and learning.

It is our hope that by connecting the best ideas of yesterday and today, it will be possible to build a bridge to what will become the essential skills of the future. A basic assumption is that all students must be educated to the point where they can successfully deal with the problems found in a brave new world. Another premise here is that any new approach to curriculum and instruction should start by examining the intersection of the best of past practice and new educational possibilities of the future.

In any era, transforming a classroom or school into a contemporary learning environment requires paying attention to consistent classroom routines, using assessment data for improvement, and having a coherent organizational structure. The old foundations of reading, writing, and mathematics and the new basics of science, technology, and the arts are at the core of schooling. More than ever, thinking about curriculum and instruction has to occur as the traditional boundaries between politics, technology, culture, education, and ecology disappear.

Change really does favor the prepared mind. Reflection, discussion, and cultivating the disposition for critical thinking can always inform and enrich our teaching. Changing school culture to accommodate a world where we are all so much more interconnected involves sharing what works across organizational and national boundaries. As changes take place, there is a natural tension between what we know and what we can imagine.

Cultural decay, global economic competition, and political lethargy have all contributed to the decline in the public sectors of American life. Even in the most favorable economic times, many communities and their schools get left behind. Although attention is paid to such modern realities, we leave plenty of room for idealism, hope, and practical ideas that will help us all develop schools worthy of our children.

The good news is that there is general agreement that the most powerful way to strengthen any society is to strengthen the schools. Also, nearly everyone agrees that the future depends on creating a better-educated, freer, and more efficient citizenry.

Predicting the future is beyond human capacity, but students can learn about the different terrains where they may find themselves living and working. Certain educational guidelines and basic principles will not disappear. For example, the curriculum has to be meaningful, make connections, emphasize responsibility, and reflect human values.

As we set out to improve schooling, it is important to recognize that change is never completed because everyone is constantly learning and experiencing insights for practice, research, and collaboration.

Change is a permanent feature of pedagogy today and will be even more so tomorrow. The days of stationary educational goals are over; learning to hit moving targets is part of today's reality. So, you can be sure that as we move farther into this century, there will be continuous waves of change flowing across any structure we build.

ONE

Introduction

Essential Skills in a Changing World

Innovation lies at the intersection of learning, imagination, and reality.
What a learner believes is possible shapes the range of possibilities.
—paraphrasing Dweck

In the last few decades we have seen major changes in everything from basic human communication to the nature of the global economy. Around the world people now recognize the fact that a nation's ability to grow and compete in the decades ahead depends on how well the next generation of innovators is educated.

Having core competencies in basic subjects still matters. What's new to the essential skills mix is the increased attention being given to skills like adaptability, resilience, critical thinking, and the ability to synthesize information.

Advances in fields like neuroscience and technology are providing new possibilities for curriculum and instruction. Although teaching and learning have taken on new dimensions, schools have not changed as much as the world around them. The capacity of educators to deal with change, learn from it, and help their students manage new ideas has a lot to do with academic success (Trilling and Fadel, 2012).

As we move farther into the new century, ever more powerful digital tools will require the schools to deal more effectively with these remarkable information and communication vehicles. To prepare for the technologies to come, it is best to be knowledgeable and engaged with what's available today.

Digital technology isn't the most powerful information and communications vehicle there is—it's just the most powerful we've discovered so far. To get some idea of where the technology is taking us, we have to

1

examine where it has come from and where it is now. So before looking ahead, it is important to look around today, and then to consider some questions about tomorrow.

- What do you think the world will be like in fifteen or twenty years?
- What kind of an education will be essential for success in tomorrow's world?
- How do you reach, engage, and teach today's generation of students?
- Where are the information and thoughts being shaped by technology taking us?

Try altering these questions or adding to the list.

Everybody in the classroom has to learn how to ask good questions before they can get useful answers.

FACING AN UNCERTAIN FUTURE WITH CONFIDENCE

Children now grow up in a fast-paced, technology-changing world that is altering how they think, learn, communicate, and socialize. Multitasking is part of today's youth picture. Although it's hard for youngsters to realize it, efficient multitasking is a myth. It simply isn't possible to do two tasks together as well as doing one separately.

Although the hyperactivity is bound to speed up, the future will unfold in unexpected directions that are quite different from anything we have known. Still, it is possible to be prepared and proactive with what's to come.

For learners at any age, education has expanded beyond classroom walls. Today's dynamic lifelong learning environment includes factors like social networks, self-driven instruction, and interactive media. So, preparing students involves making sure that they are enthusiastic about lifelong learning and view it as a natural part of day-to-day life.

The digital age is altering how we all think, communicate, and socialize in a distracted world. But whether it's today or tomorrow, it is clear that both active face-to-face learning and modern technologies have the potential to amplify whatever is going on in the classroom. Still, turning that potential into a positive reality on a large scale depends on our educational vision, teacher preparation, a well-designed curriculum, and the ability to respond to rapid change (Collins, 2009).

Although intellectually connected social and technological skills matter, uncertainties are multiplying as we progress through the decades ahead. But no matter what surprises crop up, you can be sure that we face a future where human communication, interaction, and learning are no longer bound by time, space, and form.

The skills students will need in the decades ahead involve core subjects, media, technology, learning, teamwork, and innovation. As far as the classroom is concerned, whatever tools the teacher decides to use must ignite student learning in a way that enhances the imagination and opens the door to innovative ideas. However educators go about their work, standards, learning environments, and professional development will all help pave the way to that future (Bellanca and Brandt, 2010).

It has become harder than ever to guess the sources from which future problems and the impulses for dramatic change will come. What *is* clear is that change favors the prepared mind and that the intellectual energy of a society matters. It is also clear that as schools prepare to greet the future, they must be able to help students collaboratively perceive, analyze, interpret, and discover a whole new range of meanings (Zmuda, 2011).

Fortunately, everything we know and value won't fade into oblivion. We now have e-books and interactive literature, but traditional paper books are an elegant user-friendly tool that won't go away. We can interact with people around the word, but we still need face-to-face cooperative group skills.

No matter how technology gets added to the mix, children will still have to read, write, and solve mathematical problems. Being able to evaluate information and take an informed position on an issue will continue to be valued. The difference is that many valued attributes are going to be applied to new media and new situations.

INSTRUCTION IN AN AGE OF RAPID TECHNOLOGICAL CHANGE

Today's information and communications technology supports global observation, interaction, and learning as never before. One result is a huge outflowing of information that contributes to shared cultural and intergenerational experiences. When these elements come together, they can help stimulate a more aesthetic and productive learning environment by combining new information-distribution possibilities with the more collaborative aspects of face-to-face learning.

The future will offer a vast array of possible combinations and surprising levels of complexity. In spite of the ceaseless assault of new ideas and technologies in the decades ahead, we can learn to be proactive. And we can live with change more productively.

As the twenty-first century moves ahead, change is ever more ubiquitous and relentless. Reality cries out for new definitions and people who can redefine themselves through lifelong learning. This includes moving continuous and active educational experiences ever closer to the center of today's life and workplace reality.

Educational models are increasingly influenced by the experimental research on instruction, subject matter standards, advancing technological possibilities, and understandings about the social nature of learning. Teachers can be sure that they will be called on to shoulder some of the responsibility for devising a curriculum that helps produce citizens who can live and work productively in ever-more dynamic and complex societies.

The atmosphere of the school, parental involvement, technology, and a standards-based curriculum all help. But there is no alternative to a high-quality teacher in the classroom. It takes well-educated teachers to help students become inner and outer learners who will connect to wider and wider circles of society. But they can't do it unless everyone—from parents to the media—takes more responsibility for the education of children.

The professionalization of teaching is one of the keys to quality schooling. Professionals have certain guidelines, but they do not follow a prepackaged script. In spite of Nietzsche's dictum, "dancing in chains" is not the highest art form. Teachers can usually make good use of some informed guidance. But they also need autonomy and flexibility. Accountability has to go hand in hand with professional decision making.

Every high-quality educational future requires putting more resources into focused learning opportunities for teachers. Efforts are under way to move from traditional in-service training models to broader notions of professional development. Perpetual staff development and school-embedded learning for teachers are bound to be important features in tomorrow's schools. The direction of teacher in-service education may be open to question, but the concept of the teacher as a lifelong learner is now a given.

SOCIAL REALITIES IN THE AGE OF INFORMATION

A clear understanding of a problem prefigures its lines of solution.
—Margaret Mead

You can't guarantee everyone a perfect family; you could guarantee them better social surroundings and better educational possibilities. Overall the environment a child grows up in is an important factor in academic success.

Caught between the challenges of new media and a culturally diverse society, educators find themselves on the edge of something new. Exactly what it is, is still a mystery. Everyday reality intrudes into schools as never before. In today's social milieu, the schools are sometimes the child's only venue for socially and intellectually stimulating work. Giving children an education sufficient for healthy and productive lives is more important than ever.

The more affluent your home and school, the more likely you are to see the imaginative side of computers and the curriculum—and the more likely students are to succeed in school. Although there are examples of quality schooling in every economic group, a child's zip code still matters. Libraries, schools, and other institutions can help students who are falling behind, but it's hard to learn about things like technology if you don't have easy access to it.

Big changes are increasingly happening before anyone really figures out what they mean. In the decades ahead, higher-order thinking skills will matter more than ever. Students will be increasingly called on to use problem solving, critical reasoning, and creative thinking skills to solve a wide range of problems (Lehrer, 2012).

> The most creative people often wander through marginal perspectives and integrate what they find and imagine. By adaptively moving through strange domains and surreal landscapes, the most productive are able to build a creative niche, market, and identity. Are such levels of creativity a gift, a thought process that can be learned, or some combination of the two? We would argue that at least on some levels, creative alertness, independence, and the ability to fill in missing pieces of a puzzle can be taught. (Lehrer, 2012)

To deal with real-world problems and stay relevant, teachers must have the resources to integrate the most powerful media into their day-to-day lessons. Once the pedagogical piece is in place, the technology can help. Every child should be able to use technological tools to explore material in a manner that sparks curiosity, encourages collaborative inquiry, and extends learning possibilities.

Intellectual and technological tools must be mastered to achieve just about anything today. Certainly teachers, parents, and the local community are directly responsible for helping young people gain the knowledge and skills necessary for success in an increasingly complex society. But everyone—from the media to the business world—shares responsibility for setting the conditions under which schooling takes place.

ATTITUDES THAT INFLUENCE EFFECTIVE TEACHING AND LEARNING

Schools can become a community of learners by creating a caring atmosphere, attending to student interests, and promoting meaningful learning. When the school culture values academic achievement and personal commitment, it helps break down barriers to learning and moves students in the direction of academic success.

Students and teachers need to be active participants in their own learning. We must all take every opportunity to recognize the impact and positive influence that teachers can have on the children's lives. A teacher's daily interactions with students are a powerful influence.

What does it take to start teaching? First of all, prospective teachers need the intellectual tools learned in the arts and sciences. Equally important, they must acquire the foundational skills that relate to strategic learning and pedagogical methods. Even the best college graduates flounder if they start teaching without a thorough knowledge of the characteristics of effective instruction. A related key to becoming a successful teacher involves early fieldwork experiences in different communities and different school settings.

Effective teachers have high expectations for their students. They also respect creative potential and develop a personal connectedness with their students. In fact, the interpersonal relationships and enthusiasm that develop over matters of content are at the heart of schooling.

Through active participation in staff development programs, teachers can work in association with peers to grow professionally and personally (David and Cuban, 2010). By cooperating to reach common goals, teachers are more likely to appreciate and respect one another. Positive attitudes make a difference. When teachers possess a positive attitude toward their teaching, they are more likely to continue their teaching career and students are more likely to achieve academic success.

Schools that involve teachers in participatory decision making and collaborative strategies for addressing school problems are most likely to reinforce a teacher's commitment to the profession. Effective staff development programs have taken this into account as they address the challenge of sustaining the long-term commitment of dedicated and committed teachers.

Experienced teachers understand that teaching is a complex undertaking that requires time. Conditions may be difficult, but effective teachers accept and enjoy the challenges of teaching. They know that they make a difference in students' lives.

Many teachers describe success in personal terms and view it as related to being personally durable and capable. Knowing the child and understanding the community are frequently mentioned as important. Most teachers who have elected to remain in their schools for more than three years feel in control of their environment and believe teaching is a rich and rewarding experience.

Effective teachers are more likely to believe that

- creating a feeling of excitement about the subject matter or skill being taught is important;
- children can always learn more and that the teachers' effort and energy are instrumental in students' learning;

- providing children the opportunity for active participatory experiences is a powerful incentive for learning;
- it is important to reflect a strong sense of personal caring about students and adjust instruction to their needs;
- children try hardest when they are fairly certain of success, but not absolutely positive;
- children learn most from teachers who believe that the level of student effort can predict achievement;
- children learn most when their questions and learning activities are connected with big ideas, key concepts, and their intellectual curiosity (Borich, 2010).

Although there are many approaches to good teaching, it is our belief that effective teachers often share some of the same characteristics.

Activity

Take a few minutes and write down a few of the teaching characteristics of your favorite teacher. Share with another person, a small group, or with the whole class. What are the similarities and differences between the above list and your favorite teacher's characteristics? See if you can change a point or add an important characteristic to the above list. Would you take something out? Remember, no human teacher is going to have all the "right" characteristics.

REVITALIZING THE PUBLIC SCHOOLS

Global competition is one thing; the future of American democracy is another. Both depend on the revitalization of the public schools. This is where the majority of American children will continue to be educated, make choices about life, and connect to youngsters from different backgrounds. It is also where images are formed of what it means to be a good person, have a good life, and live in a good society.

The interpreting and reinterpreting of the ideal of universal public education will be with us in the decades ahead. Small-scale private-sector experiments are fine, but to reach the majority of students, innovations must reach successfully into the public sector.

Large-scale educational change requires a sustained public commitment. Once this is in place, we must involve a widespread cadre of public school educators who are willing to implement new approaches to instruction. The goal should be nothing less than transforming all of the nation's schools into a world-class system. Ideally, curriculum designs should build on national traditions, values, and culture—while helping the schools carry out rigorous self-examinations, vigorous innovations, and a commitment to greater effectiveness.

Change won't come easily. Transforming schools will occasionally require fighting state and district systems that are hostile to change. In a few schools, students are still made to feel unwelcome, intellectually inadequate, uncomfortable, and bored. At the earliest opportunity, they drop out.

Over one million students a year leave school before graduation. For some who stay, schools may offer little encouragement for those who have talents extending beyond the ability to manipulate words and numbers. In spite of the grim social realities that weigh heavily on the shoulders of some children, the right kind of educational support can make a permanent difference.

EDUCATION, CULTURE, AND LEADERSHIP

Culture may be viewed as a coherent system of attitudes, values, and institutions that influence both individual and group behavior. The idea of culture has become ever more elastic and blurred by modern communications, swift transport, and the breakdown of traditional societies.

Cultures that nurture the human creative capacity across age groups usually do better than those that don't. When education is thought of as a continuum from prenatal care through adult life, it is bound to have a more powerful effect. Any attack on American social and educational problems must fight uphill against profound social trends. Clearly, we must make some drastic changes in our educational system to remain competitive internationally. Balancing an understanding of globalization with the unifying ideas of democracy and social responsibility is a desirable educational goal.

New technologies like computers, satellites, and the Internet are able to weave the world together as never before. Like books, the latest technology can be used in smart ways to support learning, or you can do time-burning stupid things with it. As far as computers and the Internet are concerned, the important thing is figuring out how they can improve student achievement, provide greater equity, and prepare students for life in the decades ahead.

Movies were the latest thing in the 1910s, radio in the 1920s, television in the 1950s, and the Internet in the 1990s (Wu, 2011). There is always something new just beyond the horizon. But whether it is some combination of television, video games, the Internet, Facebook, or anything else, if a society doesn't exercise thought and scrutiny over new technological tools, it will become ever more terrible and affect us in ever more terrible ways.

The optimistic and self-congratulatory high-technology industry may have to step back from its chaotic advance into an uncertain technological future and debate the issues surrounding the inherently negative possibilities of rapidly evolving technologies.

Whiz-bang media and peer culture can get in the way, but parents are an important ingredient in a child's education. Academic achievement is strongly influenced by the level of insistence on the part of parents that children take their studies seriously. In today's world, many parents aren't able to help. They need assistance in learning child-rearing competencies and forming social support networks. Schools often find themselves teaching the parents and the children.

Fundamental change in schools requires fundamental changes in society. The hard questions must be asked and the uncomfortable issues dealt with. For schools to make a major impact on childhood difficulties requires parallel changes in cultural beliefs, social incentives, the status of teachers, and basic notions about schooling.

Limiting the educational focus to concerns like national testing and school choice avoids the more crucial issues of moral numbness, individualism degenerating into greed, spiritual alienation, social injustice, or the diminishing prospects for a healthy future. For too long, we have not worried enough about future generations, nor met our obligations to one another.

When it comes to improving the schools, it isn't just about money; it's values, willingness to sacrifice, and the ability to look at children and young adults in their totality. To deal with many of the issues most important to a child's future, teachers will have to educate in ways that haven't been fully conceived of yet. It may not be possible to change yesterday's mistakes, but it is possible to change the future. It takes leadership that is willing to address the issues of our time in a bold manner — to inspire, instill, trust, and carry out carefully conceived plans. Leaders don't just reflect the health or ailment of a society; they help create them.

At the school district level, long-term leadership with high expectations is important. In good districts, the attitude is, "We can teach anybody to learn." At the principal's level, success is often attributed to having latitude in curricular and spending decisions. Other positive factors include having tangible goals, careful teacher recruitment, and parent outreach programs.

AN ERA OF ACCELERATION, INTEGRATION, AND CHANGE

Expressions of scientific knowledge in better technology are now global in their effect. Science and its technological tools have directly accounted for fundamental changes in the world economy and at the same time, tied the world together by nearly instantaneous communication. From genetic engineering to the Internet, science and its associates are now in a position to direct and manipulate the world more than ever. We have only a dim glimpse of the world ahead.

Genetics, robotics, and nanotechnologies are just three of the newer technologies that pose a potential risk to the physical world. The possibility of people being able to order out for private futures is one ethical problem. Machines that can self-replicate and nanotechnologies are another. From the genetic shaping of individuals to digital experiences bought off the shelf, it is becoming easier to create natural facts (like new species or molecules).

The dynamic and compelling force of information and communication technology is becoming more effective at creating virtual realities. These made-to-order worlds are bound to take time away from face-to-face human interaction and ordinary sensory experiences.

Schools can temper some of the harsh edges of technology by becoming good role models by connecting the social aspects of learning with broader online communities. They can also enhance learning with dynamic visual representations of concepts and media production (videos, Web sites, social networks, etc.). Along the way, educators will have to restructure the teaching and learning role and make sure that assessment practices are aligned with the curriculum.

The revolution in how information is provided is one of the greatest cultural changes in history. To extend the idea of what is possible is to change the way people think and the way they act. The communication revolution is more than a technological advance; it is a major factor in spreading new ways of thinking. For a jump of comparable importance, you have to go back to the transformation of culture, thinking, and learning that was caused by the introduction of the printing press. Our schools must reflect these new realities.

Technology, economics, and culture are increasingly tied together. Now we truly live in one world. The interaction among events and trends in all parts of the world would not be possible without the communications that have rapidly tied humanity together with a new immediacy and intimacy. More than ever, global change is driven by new technologies that have taken on a speed of their own. The result of fewer and fewer certainties is the demand for ever-higher levels of education and competency.

The word *inertia* is often associated with attempts to change the curriculum. Teacher attitudes, the need to reeducate students, traditional ways of doing things, and assessment practices all get in the way of initiating a new curriculum while operating an old system. Test taking and test preparation are but a couple of examples of how efforts to improve the schools can sometimes have the opposite effect.

We are still learning how to capitalize on schools' social character to contribute to healthy educational growth. Not staying up to date is to fall behind; therefore, one of the most important features of a successful educational system is the capacity for self-renewal and continuous change. There are speed bumps on the way to new practices: teacher preparation, the need to reeducate students, assessment practices, and the fact that new arrangements have to be put in place while operating the old system.

Abundant national resources, temperate climate conditions, location, and good education levels all play a role in national development. Whatever may be said about American education and competitiveness, Americanization remains one of the main vehicles for modernity. As the country that benefits most from global economic integration, the United States has a national interest in making sure that economic progress is sustainable for as many people in as many countries as possible.

We have the tools to make a difference. Taking responsibility for striking the right balance between globalization's humanizing aspects and its dehumanizing tenancies is another question. A certain respect for other approaches to modernity would be healthy.

A shared goal of educators is developing scientifically grounded approaches that meet the diverse cognitive, social, and academic needs of students. So, it is important to develop strategies and activities that maximize subject matter engagement, reasoning, and creative potential. These twenty-first-century skills are directly related to the ability to gather information and find patterns that help organize perceptions.

By linking content and the imagination, we can move in the direction of answering some of the deepest questions.

ESSENTIAL SKILLS IN THE KNOWLEDGE AGE

Education has an increasingly crucial role to play in a globalized knowledge society. Improving schooling takes a sustained societal commitment to improving education and the student's environment outside school. The world outside the classroom is changing more rapidly than ever; some of these changes are for the good while some are for the worse.

One of the keys to successful schooling is the creation of learning communities where students are active and collaborative participants in the construction of meaning. There are solid examples of positive educational change around the country and around the world. The challenge is to take the best practices and give teachers the resources to make this change happen everywhere.

The media and others outside the education field can help by doing more to promote teaching as a noble profession that is the key to a successful democracy.

Fortunately for teachers, many of today's basic pedagogical principles remain constant. For example, activities involving reasoning, collaboration, and communication will still matter. It's just that tomorrow's schools will pay even closer attention to making sure that these elements influence teaching and learning for understanding.

Whether it is today or tomorrow, good teachers will be adapting their lessons by providing a variety of ways to learn. This involves a continuous process of "finding new ways to deal with time, space, materials, groups, and strategies that balance content requirements with multiple pathways for learning" (Tomlinson and Imbeau, 2010).

Schools can build on the potential of new technology, but genuine education depends on personal interaction among people and ideas in an aesthetically and intellectually stimulating environment. Whether it's in school or in the workplace, learning activities completed in small face-to-face groups can make the classroom environment more lively and interesting for everyone.

Learning in direct association with others will not be diminished in any recognizable future. Technology accelerates everything. But no matter how many whiz-bang gadgets we invent, direct social interaction will continue to be a key element in achieving competency in basic subject matter and supporting twenty-first-century skills.

SUMMARY, CONCLUSION, AND LOOKING TO THE FUTURE

Teaching is both an art and a science; the foundations are built on an understanding of the characteristics of effective instruction. Like everything else, the future of schooling will depend on new ideas. To some extent, this requires rethinking both what and how students learn.

There is general agreement that when teachers match up-to-date themes with content skills, they are more likely to generate relevant and powerful learning experiences. It is also clear that a deep understanding of core subjects has to go hand in hand with developing the imaginative skills that will be so important in the decades ahead (Coates, 2010).

Both subject matter and creative imagination have a lot to do with enhancing a student's ability to follow up on his or her curiosity. Helping students develop intellectual curiosity is more than getting them to come up with the right answer. It requires making sure that learners are fully engaged with thinking, experimenting, and interacting with others. Routine drill and practice, tied to a multibillion-dollar testing industry, simply isn't enough to make sure that schools are quality organizations.

By matching instruction to the times in which we live, it is more likely that students will be prepared for changes happening today, tomorrow, and beyond. Children are naturals when it comes to identifying and solving problems in a world where nothing is complete. They quickly learn that what matters most is the direction of movement.

The ability to deal with ambiguity, prior knowledge, personal interests, and the ability to communicate what is being learned are all part of today's skills package. The same can be said for learning to drink from a technological fire hose of information and sort out what is important.

Although strict control is beyond any of us, we can all help plot the trajectory of change. As far as educators are concerned, it is possible to make contributions to the changing nature of curriculum and instruction. Along the way, teachers and their students are bound to influence the changing nature of an increasingly interconnected world. At any age, making a contribution really matters, even if it's on a small scale—anyone involved should feel fortunate as he or she helps shape the future.

Along the path to the future, we should be able to conduct ourselves in a way that reflects our hopes, dreams, and values. By building on the best possibilities, teachers and students can link arms to reach past whatever obstacles get thrown in the way and achieve models of success in an increasingly interconnected world.

> Language makes us human
> Science and technology make us powerful
> The arts refine our thinking
> Living in community with others can set us free
> —D. Adams

SUGGESTED RESOURCES

Darling-Hammond, L. (1997). *The right to learn: A blueprint for creating schools that work.* San Francisco: Jossey-Bass.

REFERENCES

Bellanca, J., and R. Brandt (Eds.). (2010). *21st century skills: Rethinking how students learn.* Bloomington, IN: Solution Tree Press.

Borich, G. (2010). *Effective teaching methods: Research-based practice.* 7th ed. Boston: Allyn & Bacon.

Coates, M. (Ed.). (2010). *Shaping a new educational landscape: Exploring possibilities for education in the 21st century (Future schools).* London: Continuum International Publishing Group.

Collins, A. (2009). *Rethinking education in the age of technology.* New York: Teachers College Press.

David, J., and L. Cuban. (2010). *Cutting through the hype: The essential guide to school reform.* Cambridge, MA: Harvard Education Press.

Dweck, C. S. (2012). *Mindset: How you can fulfill your potential.* London: Constable & Robinson.

Lehrer, J. (2012). *Imagine: How creativity works.* Boston: Houghton Mifflin Harcourt.

Tomlinson, C., and M. Imbeau. (2010). *Leading and managing a differentiated classroom.* Alexandria, VA: Association for Supervision and Curriculum Development.

Trilling, B., and C. Fadel. (2012). *21st century skills: Learning for life in our times.* San Francisco: Jossey-Bass Education.

Wu, T. (2011). *The master switch: The rise and fall of information empires.* New York: Alfred A. Knopf.

Zmuda, A. (2011). *Breaking free from myths about teaching and learning: Innovation as an engine for student success.* Alexandria, VA: Association for Supervision and Curriculum Development.

TWO

Thinking and Learning in a Technologically Intensive World

Out of the questions of students come most of the creative ideas and discoveries. —Ellen Langer

The ability to deal with the convergence of thinking and technological tools is one of the keys to success in the twenty-first century. Take the Internet as an example. It can help us extend our thinking and our connection to others. It may also be the biggest distraction to come along since television. The difference between useful and useless has a lot to do with learning how to use digital technologies and their associates with a measure of wisdom.

Today's information technology is a force that can expand or contract human potential. New technologies affect nearly every aspect of our life and require new ways of thinking. Emerging technology frequently opens up the possibility of imaginative solutions and alternative paths to the future. So it is little wonder that educational systems around the world look for ways to produce more thoughtful innovators and informed knowledge workers.

A good metaphor for how to teach thinking skills might be found in the difference between a sponge and panning for gold. The sponge approach emphasizes fairly passive knowledge acquisition; the panning for gold approach stresses active interaction with knowledge as it is being acquired (Dede and Richards, 2012). Whatever combination of approaches is taken, developing the ability to think clearly, creatively, and critically is an important part of education today.

Here, creative and critical thinking are viewed as overlapping concepts. Creative thinking tends to look at problems or situations from an imaginative perspective and suggests fresh solutions. Students might be

15

stimulated by methods ranging from brainstorming to the step-by-step processes of lateral thinking (O'Toole and Beckett, 2009). Critical thinking often involves a persistent effort to examine information in light of reliable evidence.

Along with carefully selected information, creative and critical reasoning can reinforce each other. Thinking transforms the information gathered by our digital devices, and that information invites thinking (Howie, 2011).

Developing approaches that extend students' thinking skills across the curriculum is a strategy that is widely supported. Both the concept and the teaching strategies associated with thinking skills can be found in just about every curriculum. Better yet, most teachers are building at least some pieces of the thinking skills puzzle into their day-to-day work.

YESTERDAY, TODAY, AND TOMORROW

We have always known that new technologies produce problems—it's just that it's hard to figure out in advance what those problems will be. Technological devices have always been part of the equation; it's just that texting, IM-ing, iPhoning, Tweeting, and the like have changed thinking in unexpected ways. Today's media, for example, have helped move thinking from a relatively calm and focused process into something that needs to take in and dole out information in short, disjointed, and overlapping bursts (Carr, 2010).

Our mobile Internet age has produced some "digital natives" who expect continuous connection and feel uneasy when expected to think in the few moments when they are truly alone (Turkle, 2011). It is little wonder that many students today have more trouble concentrating or thinking intelligently when they spend so much time skimming one surface after another to the point of distraction.

As far as thoughtful behavior is concerned, it is time to think about where technology belongs and put it in its place. In spite of the negatives, it is still possible that as technology continues to improve, the benefits of our new media tools can be shaped in a way that outweighs the drawbacks. With or without digital technology, most educators favor paying close attention to thinking and reasoning.

The educational path that was developed in the early twentieth century stressed the behaviorist view of learning. What could be seen was behavior. Learning was looked at as changed behavior. Lacking the knowledge of what goes on inside the thinking process, the behaviorists measured behaviors and learned to alter them with behavior reinforcers (rewarding positive behaviors, punishing negative actions).

As behaviorism faded from the scene, cognitive science filled the void. Most educators welcomed the change. Cognition may be thought of as the process of knowing. Cognitive science included a wide range of human activities: critical thinking, making judgments, decision making, and creative thinking. Cognitive science also moved the ball in the direction of constructivism, the basic idea being that the thinking individual does not simply take in knowledge, but is actively involved in constructing that knowledge.

In the classroom, good teaching encourages students to actively construct knowledge within lessons that have clear goals, that allow for guided practice, and that provide ongoing assessment. Also, leaving some room for student choice amplifies critical and creative thinking.

MEANINGFUL CRITICAL AND CREATIVE THINKING

The thinking of every child can be enhanced if the learning is *challenging;* this means that in addition to providing proof of new facts and experiences, there must also be *group feedback.* Challenges can be as simple as presenting original content, including journal writing and hands-on materials. It's important to often change teaching strategies, to apply computer programs, to have students work in groups, to give students choice when doing projects, and to take field trips.

Student feedback should not be overlooked. This builds confidence, reduces stress, and increases thinking's coping abilities. Students' peers are the greatest stimuli in the classroom. Collaborative groups provide students with a sense of feeling valued and cared for.

Thinking is a search for meaning, a purposeful quest for understanding and clarity. This journey often provides new points of view and solutions to problems. Thinking is intentional, purposeful, and deliberate. Individuals can be resourceful and adventuresome. Stimulating their students' critical and creative imagination is one of the most important teaching challenges teachers face today.

Thinking is built on personal experiences. It is also influenced by emotions, culture, home environment, and educational possibilities. Critical and creative thinking experiences express original ideas and solutions. They have a conscious and mental focus. The playful spirit of creative thinking can occur while day dreaming, fantasizing, or just having an idea while taking a hike along a trail. Creative thinking extends art and beauty as it reaches beyond the adequate to try elegant solutions.

Critical thinking is constructing meaning by observing, interpreting, analyzing, and manipulating information in response to a problem. Clarifying and solving problems, pondering alternatives, strategically planning, and analyzing the results are all activities that support critical thinking. *Creative thinking* is flowing, flexible, novel, and detailed. Creative thinking skills try to create novel expressions, unique conceptions, and original approaches. The mental power to see things in an unusual and imaginative way is linked with problem solving and is part of critical thinking.

As teachers encourage the original ideas developed by children, it is important to remember that many problems of the future will be solved by people who are flexible, open, unique, and actively productive. Critical and creative thinking means being able to choose alternative explanations and show intellectual curiosity in a manner that is flexible and unique.

Critical thinking lessons might include having students analyze the hidden assumptions that produce meanings and different results of data information. Such intellectually demanding thinking helps students identify, clarify, and solve problems. The questions explored can be as general as, "Can we be certain about the knowledge of this subject?" Questions can be as simple as, "How was that done?" or "What does that mean?"

T. S. Eliot maintained that genuine poetry communicates before it's understood. The wording may be changed. Students are never too young to analyze the underlying assumptions that influence meaning. And they are never too young to question the explanations of findings and participate in the act of knowledge creation. We listen to what David Whyte said: "The eddies and swells of everyday experience." He uses poetry to finish his point: "I turned my face for a moment and it became my life" (p. 231).

TEACHING, LEARNING, AND THINKING HABITS

Understanding the relationship between theory, research, and practice is the foundation of pedagogical knowledge. The content standards build on this cycle to give a coherent, professionally defensible conception of how a subject can be framed for instruction. They do not put forward one best way to teach subject matter *or* thinking skills. Instead, all the standards projects have left room for interpretation.

A good place to start with students centers around real-life experiences that evoke personal meaning. Across all subjects, high-quality lessons often begin with real materials and make use of interactive learning in a way that allows students to explore the many dimensions of thoughtfulness, subject matter, and real-world applications. The basic idea is to help students form a new set of expectations and create a new sense of understanding. Asking the right questions certainly helps (Browne and Keeley, 2009).

We all make sense of something by connecting to a set of personal everyday experiences. Good teachers have always connected educational goals to practical problem solving and students' life experiences. This way, thinking skills are introduced into the curriculum so that students are intensely involved in reasoning, elaboration, forming hypotheses, and problem solving. New ideas of literacy will have to move beyond disciplinary boundaries.

Evolving mature thinkers who are able to acquire and use knowledge involves educating minds rather than training memories. Often the acquisition of advanced thinking skills is well structured and planned; other times it's a chance encounter. Raising thoughtful questions about what's being viewed, heard, or read is a dimension of thinking that makes a meaningful contribution. When encouraged to think intelligently, students often come up with good decisions and elegant solutions. As all these elements come together, they shape the core of effective thinking and learning.

Using new methods for teaching mathematics, science, the arts, and language arts depends on reflective teachers. This means that both beginning and veteran teachers should take courses in learning math and science through inquiry and learn to apply the arts and language arts concepts within a context similar to the one they will arrange for their students. The result enlarges horizons and organizational possibilities.

Creative and critical thinking are natural human processes that can be extended by awareness and practice. Both critical and creative thinking employ specific core thinking skills. Classroom instructional practice in the development of these skills might include the following:

1. Be accurate, clear, open-minded, and sensitive to others; defend a position.
2. Engage in difficult problems, extend the limits of your knowledge, find new ways to look at situations outside conventional boundaries, dare to imagine, innovate, and trust.
3. Listen with understanding when listening to other people and try to understand their points of view. This is one of the highest forms of communication.
4. Be aware of your thinking: be sensitive to feedback, and plan and evaluate your actions. Take your time, remain calm, think before you act.
5. Be attentive. This includes skills such as observing, getting information, forming questions, and using inquiry.
6. Pose clear questions in easy-to-understand language.
7. Remain open to continuous learning.
8. Analyze and form hunches. Analysis is at the heart of critical and creative thinking. This includes recognizing and articulating attributes and focusing on details and structure, identifying relationships and patterns, and finding errors.
9. Use models and metaphors: such higher-order thinking as making comparisons, using metaphors, producing analogies, and providing explanations.

10. Gather data and assess and evaluate ideas. This establishes criteria or verifies data.
11. Take risks. Elegant solutions often demand risk taking and thinking independently.
12. Search out humor. This frees creativity and stimulates higher thinking skills. People who initiate humor are verbally playful when interacting with others; they thrive on being able to laugh at situations and themselves.
13. Every inquiry, if explored with enthusiasm and with care, will use some of these core thinking skills (Jacobs, 2004).

ILLUMINATING LEARNING BY TEACHING FOR THOUGHTFULNESS

The multidimensional search for meaning is made at least a little easier when there is a supportive group climate for generating questions and investigating possibilities. Critical thinking questions may also come into play after solutions are put forward. Ask students to analyze problems they have solved. As they examine how underlying assumptions influence interpretations, children can be pulled more deeply into a topic. And by evaluating their findings on the basis of logic, they invite other possibilities.

To have power over the story that dominates one's life in these technologically intensive times means having the power to retell it, deconstruct it, joke about it, and change it as times change. Without this power, it is more difficult to think and act on new thoughts and open the doors to deep thinking.

The old view of teaching as the transmission of content has been expanded to include new intellectual tools and new ways of helping students thoughtfully construct knowledge on their own and with peers. Teachers who invite thoughtfulness understand that knowledge is to be shared or developed rather than held by the authority. They arrange instruction so that children construct concepts and develop their thinking skills. As a result, everyone involved becomes an active constructor of knowledge and more capable of making thoughtful decisions in the future.

Recognizing the development of thinking skills is a good first step toward its application and assessment. Beyond specific teaching strategies, the climate of the classroom and the behavior of the teacher are very important. Teachers need to model critical thinking behaviors—setting the tone, atmosphere, and environment for learning. Being able to collaborate with other teachers can make a formative contribution in how the teacher might better see and construct individual classroom reality.

In collaborative problem solving, teachers can help one another in the clarification of goals. They also share the products of their joint imaginations. Thus, perceptions are changed, ideas flow, and practice can be meaningfully strengthened, deepened, and extended. Like their students, teachers can become active constructors of knowledge.

A curriculum that ignores the powerful ideas of its charges will miss many opportunities for illuminating knowledge. To teach content without regard for self-connected thinking prevents subject matter knowledge from being transformed in the student's mind. If the curriculum is to be viewed as enhancing being and opening to the unfamiliar—rather than merely imparting knowledge and skills—then reasoned decision making is part of the process.

Taking student thinking seriously is more likely to be successful in cultivating thoughtfulness and subject matter competence. Respecting unique thought patterns can also be viewed as a commitment to caring communication and openness.

Encouraging fresh ideas or opposing views is often difficult for administrators. All of us need the occasional push or encouragement to get out of a rut. Breaking out of established patterns can be done collectively or individually. But it takes those most directly involved to make it happen.

JOURNEYS OF DISCOVERY

It is important for all of us to develop our own reflection and inquiry skills—becoming students of our own thinking. For example, when teachers decide to participate with students in learning to think on a daily basis, they nourish human possibilities. Can teachers make a difference? Absolutely. The idea is to connect willing teachers with innovative methods and materials so that they can build learning environments that are sensitive to students' growing abilities to think for themselves.

By promoting thoughtful learning across the full spectrum of personalities, cultures, and ways of knowing, teachers can make a tremendous difference and perform a unique service for the future.

When the ideal and the actual are linked, the result can produce a dynamic, productive, and resilient form of learning. What we know about teaching and thinking is increasingly being put into practice in model classrooms and schools. These exemplary programs recognize that powerful inquiry can help students make personal and group discoveries that change thinking. Good thinking skills can turn an unexamined belief into a reasoned one.

By nurturing informed thinking and awareness, we can all learn how to actively apply knowledge, solve problems, and enhance conceptual understanding across social boundaries. As children use reason and logic to change their own theories and beliefs, they grow in ways that are personally meaningful. Understanding the essence of contradictory points of view means understanding some of the universal truths that speak to everyone. A diversity of new voices can add vigor to understanding the world and our place in it.

As students learn about the perspectives of other cultures—including social and historical background—they can explore where stereotypes come from. With a little homework, each student can design a large graphic family tree to share. This way each student's cultural background can serve as a valuable tool for learning about themselves, their cultural background, and how their communities connect to others around the world.

With the globalization of media and business, it becomes ever more important to see how events in the United States affect people in other countries—and vice versa. Gaining a global perspective means developing a more integrative understanding of the human community and overlapping cultural experiences. As teachers learn to thoughtfully view the world from multiple perspectives, the way is cleared for them to become more sensitive to variation and more capable of reaching diverse learners.

DISCOVERING RELATIONSHIPS AND INVENTING NEW PERSPECTIVES

Recognizing the fact that thinking skills are key to successful learning doesn't come as a surprise to most teachers. In science, for example, you formulate hypotheses, organize experiments, collect data, analyze, interpret the findings, and solve problems. As scholars who are doing original work in any field will tell you, the reality is far less clear-cut and tidy. There are many false starts and detours as the scholars work through alternatives to discover relationships and invent new perspectives. What makes it satisfying for many scholars is the sheer power of searching at the frontiers of knowledge. This passion for inquiry and reaching outward into the unknown (for new experiences) is just as important for children.

Critical and creative thinkers tend to be reflective, flexible, and curious; they think problems through and consider original solutions. They pose and expand on new questions. The research evidence suggests that providing students with multiple perspectives and entry points into subject matter increases thinking and learning (Willis, 2006). As each of the standards projects point out in its own way, notions about how students learn a subject need to be pluralized. Almost any important concept can be approached from multiple entry points, thus emphasizing understanding and making meaningful interdisciplinary connections.

Today's schools are incorporating frameworks for literacy and learning that build on the multiple ways of thinking and representing knowledge. By organizing lessons that respect multiple entry points to knowledge, teachers can enhance thoughtfulness and make the classroom a rich environment for inquiry. By fusing the personalization of learning to achieving an attainable level of literacy across the curriculum, teachers can lay a powerful foundation for learning.

We now have diverse models of thoughtful schooling to choose from. If many of today's dreams, possibilities, and admired efforts are going to be put into widespread practice, then we all must be more courageous in helping move good practice from the educational margins and into the schools.

A child's thinking ability evolves through a dynamic of personal abilities, social values, academic subjects, and out-of-school experiences. Although teachers are usually the ones held accountable, everyone is involved (directly or indirectly) in the education of children.

Revitalizing the educational process means recognizing the incomplete models of how the world works that children bring to school with them. From birth, children are busy making sense of their environment. They do this by curiously grappling with the confusing, learning ways of understanding, developing schemes for thinking, and finding meaning.

Discipline and imaginative thought may seem antithetical, but discipline without thoughtfulness is sterile—and creative energy without discipline aborts its image.

As they begin school, children can tell stories, sing songs, and use their own processes of reasoning and intuiting to understand their surroundings. They have already developed a rich body of knowledge about the world around them by the time they reach first grade.

This natural learning process can be extended in school when a teacher is committed to critical thinking throughout the year. It is important to pay attention and work with students' natural rhythms, but it takes learning-centered instruction to continue the process of developing mature thinkers. Cognitive science was partly responsible, as were perspectives on multiple intelligences.

TOWARD A NEW VISION OF INTELLIGENCE (MULTIPLE
INTELLIGENCES)

Learning has a lot to do with finding your own gifts (Armstrong, 2009). To make learning more accessible to children means respecting multiple ways of making meaning.

The brain has a multiplicity of functions and voices that speak independently and distinctly for different individuals. Howard Gardner's framework for multiple entry points to knowledge has made an impact on the content standards. There are many differences, but each set of content standards is built on a belief in the uniqueness of each child and the view that this can be fused with a commitment to achieving worthwhile goals.

Lessons built on Gardner's ideas prove helpful in providing alternative paths for learning.

Multiple Intelligences

1. Linguistic intelligence: the capacity to use language to express ideas, excite, convince, and convey information. Speaking, writing, and reading.
2. Logical-mathematical intelligence: the ability to explore patterns and relationships by manipulating objects or symbols in an orderly manner.
3. Musical intelligence: the capacity to think in music, the ability to perform, compose, or enjoy a musical piece. Rhythm, beat, tune, melody, and singing.
4. Spatial intelligence: the ability to understand and mentally manipulate a form or object in a visual or spatial display. Maps, drawings, and media.
5. Bodily-kinesthetic intelligence: the ability to use motor skills in sports, performing arts, or art productions, particularly dance or acting.
6. Interpersonal intelligence: the ability to work in groups. Interacting, sharing, leading, following, and reaching out to others.
7. Intrapersonal intelligence: the ability to understand one's inner feelings, dreams, and ideas. Introspection, meditation, reflection, and self-assessment.
8. Naturalist intelligence: the ability to discriminate among living things (plants, animals) as well as hold a sensitivity to the natural world (Gardner, 1997).

Gardner defines intelligence as the ability to solve problems, generate new problems, and do things that are valued within one's own culture. MI (multiple intelligences) theory suggests that these eight "intelligences" work together in complex ways. Most people can develop an adequate level of competency in all of them. And there are many ways to be "intelligent" within each category.

Will the "intelligences" that were so important in the twentieth century be as central to the twenty-first?

It is possible to take issue with Gardner's approach on several points, like not fully addressing spiritual and artistic modes of thought. Although it is a distortion of MI theory, for some it's a short leap from preferred ways of learning to learning styles. Still, there is general agreement on a central point: *intelligence is not a single capacity that every human being possesses to a greater or lesser extent.*

There *are* multiple ways of knowing and learning. And whether or not we subscribe to MI theory, methods of instruction should reflect different ways of knowing. Working out the ecology of teaching for thoughtfulness requires taking risks with a wide range of bold and explicit insights.

Suggestions for Using Multiple Intelligence Activities

1. Put multiple intelligence theory into action. Some possibilities:

linguistic intelligence
write an article
develop a newscast
make a plan
describe a procedure
write a letter
conduct an interview
write a play
interpret a text or piece of writing

musical intelligence
sing a rap song
give a musical presentation
explain musical similarities
play a musical instrument
demonstrate rhythmic patterns

logical-mathematical intelligence
design and conduct an experiment
describe patterns
make up analogies to explain
solve a problem

spatial intelligence
illustrate, draw, paint, sketch
create a slide show, videotape
chart, map, or graph
create a piece of art

bodily-kinesthetic intelligence
use creative movement
design task or puzzle cards
build or construct something
bring hands-on materials to demonstrate
use the body to persuade, console or support others

interpersonal intelligence
conduct a meeting
participate in a service project
teach someone
use technology to explain
advise a friend or fictional character

naturalist intelligence
prepare an observation notebook
describe changes in the environment
care for pets, wildlife, gardens, or parks
use binoculars, telescopes, or microscopes
photograph natural objects

intrapersonal intelligence
write a journal entry
describe one of your values
assess your work
set and pursue a goal
reflect on or act out emotions

2. Build on students' interests.

When students do research either individually or with a group, allow them to choose a project that appeals to them. Students should also choose the best way for communicating their understanding of the topic. In this way, students discover more about their interests, concerns, learning styles, and intelligences.

3. Plan interesting lessons. There are many ways to plan interesting lessons.

LESSON PLANNING

1. Set the tone of the lesson. Focus student attention and relate the lesson to what students have done before. Stimulate interest.
2. Present the objectives and purpose of the lesson. What are students supposed to learn? Why is it important?
3. Provide background information: what information is available? Resources such as books, journals, videos, pictures, maps, charts, teacher lecture, class discussion, or seat work should be listed.
4. Define procedures: what are students supposed to do? This includes examples and demonstrations as well as working directions.
5. Monitor students' understanding. During the lesson, the teacher should check students' understanding and adjust the lesson if necessary. Teachers should invite questions and ask for clarification. A continuous feedback process should be in place.
6. Provide guided practice experiences. Students should have a chance to use the new knowledge presented under direct teacher supervision.
7. It is equally important that students get opportunities for independent practice where they can use their new knowledge and skills.
8. Evaluating and assessing students' work is necessary to show that students have demonstrated an understanding of significant concepts. Paper-and-pencil tests do not adequately measure students' critical and creative thinking. Observing students' behavior and their interaction with the teacher and peers is often more effective and revealing. Portfolios represent the cutting edge of more authentic and meaningful assessment. They are powerful assessment tools that require students to select, collect, and reflect on what they are creating and accomplishing.

A Sample MI Lesson Plan

Lesson Title: How Intelligence Cells Work

Students should develop understandings of personal health, changes in environments, and local challenges in science and technology. The human body and the brain are fascinating areas of study. The brain, like the rest of the body, is composed of cells; but brain cells are different from other cells (Tough, 2012). This lesson focuses on the science standards of inquiry, life science, science and technology, and personal and social perspectives.

Lesson Goals

The basic goal is to provide a dynamic experience with each of the eight "intelligences" and map out a group on construction paper.

Procedures

1. Divide the class into groups. Assign each group an intelligence.
2. Allow students time to prepare an activity that addresses their intelligence. Each small group will give a three-minute presentation (with large map) to the entire class.

Objective

To introduce students to the terminology of intelligence and to how intelligence functions, specifically, the function of intelligence cells.

Grade Level

With modifications, K–8.

Materials

Paper, pens, markers

Intelligence (Thinking) "Recipe"

5 cups of instant potato flakes, 5 cups of hot water, 2 cups of sand, pour into a 1 gallon Ziploc bag
Combine all ingredients, mix thoroughly. It should weigh about 3 pounds and have the consistency of a real part of our thinking process in our head.

Background Information

No one understands exactly how thinking works. But scientists know the answer lies within the billions of tiny cells, called *nerve cells*, that make up the thinking process. All the body's feelings and thoughts are caused by the electrical and chemical signals passing from one neuron to the next. A nerve cell looks like a tiny octopus, but with many more tentacles (some have several thousand). Nerve cells carry signals throughout our thinking process; this allows us to move, hear, see, taste, smell, remember, feel, and think.

Procedure

1. Make a model of the thinking process to show to the class. The teacher displays the thinking process and says, "The smell of a flower, the memory of a walk in the park, the pain of stepping on a nail—these experiences are made possible by the three pounds of tissue in our heads—OUR THINKING PROCESS."
2. Show a picture of the nerve cell and mention its various parts.
3. Have students label the parts of the cell and color if desired.

Activity 1: Message Transmission: Explaining How Thinking (Nerve) Cells Work

A message traveling in the nervous system of our intelligence can go 200 miles per hour (mph). These signals are transmitted from intelligence cell to cell across a connection. To understand this system, have students act out the thinking cell process.

1. Instruct students to get into groups of five. Each group should choose a group leader.
2. Direct students to stand up and form a circle. Each person is going to be an intelligence or a thinking cell. Students should be an arm's length away from the next person.
3. When the group leader says "go," have one person from the group start the signal transmission by slapping the hand of the adjacent person. The second person then slaps the hand of the next, and so on until the signal goes all the way around the circle and the transmission is complete.

Explanation: The hand that receives the slap is the branching part of the nerve cell. The middle part of the student's body is the cell body. The arm that gives the slap to the next person is the nerve cell and the hand that gives the slap is the nerve cell terminal. Between the hands of two people is the nerve connector.

Inquiry Questions

As the activity progresses, questions will arise: What are parts of a thinking nerve cell? A tiny nerve cell is one of billions that make up the thinking process. A nerve cell has three basic parts: the *nerve cell*, the *cell body*, and the *nerve cell connector*. Have students make a simple model by using their hand and spreading their fingers wide. The hand represents the cell body, the fingers represent the parts that bring information to the cell body, and the arm represents the cell connector, which takes information away from the cell body. Just as students wiggle their fingers, the nerve cells are constantly moving as they seek information. If an intelligence cell needs to send a message to another cell, the message is sent out through the nerve cell. The wrist and forearm represent the cell body. When a cell sends information down its cell body to communicate with another nerve cell, it never actually touches the other cell. The message goes from the nerve cell of the sending cell to another nerve cell by "swimming" through the space called the *cell connector*. Neuroscientists define *learning* as *two nerve cells communicating with each other*. They say that nerve cells have "learned" when one cell sends a message to another cell.

Activity 2: Connect the Dots

This activity is to show the complexity connections of the thinking process.

1. Have students draw ten dots on one side of a sheet of typing paper and ten dots on the other side of the paper.
2. Tell students to imagine that these dots represent nerve cells; assume each cell makes connections with the ten dots on the other side.
3. Then connect each dot on side one with the dots on the other side. This is quite a simplification. Each nerve cell (dot) may actually make thousands of connections with other cells.

Another part of this activity is teaching intelligence songs to students:

"I've Been Working on My Thinking"
(sung to the tune of "I've Been Working on the Railroad")

I've been working on my thinking, all the livelong day.
I've been working on my thinking, just to make my genius play.
Can't you hear my thinking snapping? Impulses bouncing to and fro,
Can't you tell that I've been learning? See how much I know!

"Because I Can Think"
(sung to the tune of "Because I Can Think")

I can flex a muscle tightly, or tap my finger lightly,

It's because I can think,
I can swim in the river, though it's cold and makes me shiver,
Just because I can think.
I am really fascinated, to be coordinated,
It's because I can think.
I can see lots of faces, feel the pain of wearing braces
Just because I can think.
Oh, I appreciate the many things that I can do,
I can taste a chicken stew, or smell perfume, or touch the dew.
I am heavy with emotion, and often have the notion,
That life is never plain.
I have lots of personality, a sense of true reality,
Because I can think.

Multiple Intelligences Learning Activities

> *Linguistic*: writing a reflection about the activity, researching how a
> nerve cell works, keeping a study journal about how nerve cells
> work
> *Bodily-Kinesthetic*: moving like a nerve cell group drama: cell signal
> transmission
> *Visual-Spatial*: mapping the connections of our thinking process (con-
> nect the dots)
> *Musical*: singing songs about nerve cells, tapping out rhythms to the
> song "Because I Can Think"
> *Naturalist*: describing changes in your thinking environment, illustrat-
> ing a thinking connection
> *Interpersonal*: participating in (acting out) a group signal nerve cell
> transmission, observing/recording
> *Intrapersonal*: reflecting on thinking, keeping a journal of how the
> brain works
> *Mathematical/Logical*: calculating nerve cell connections

Evaluation

Each group will write a reflection on the activity. Journal reflections
should tell what the students learned about thinking and how that helps
them understand how the thinking process works.

BRAIN RESEARCH AND LEARNING

Human intelligence, across all age groups, is malleable and stable enough
for learning to occur and solidify into wisdom. Thousands of new nerve
cells form every day and migrate into areas that influence thinking and
decision making. If a steady stream of new thinking cells is continually

arriving to be integrated into new circuitry, then our thinking is even more malleable than had been thought of in the past. Research now suggests that the thinking process remains remarkably plastic and we retain the ability to learn throughout our lives (Jossey-Bass, 2008).

Brain researchers have found that a small well-connected region of our thinking process is in charge of organizing and coordinating information, acting like a global workspace for solving problems. Neuroscientists also emphasize that thinking is extremely plastic and dynamic, very responsive to experience, and is an "ever-changing place"(Schank, 2011).

INTELLECTUAL TOOLS OF THE FUTURE

Since it is so difficult to figure out what knowledge will be crucial to students in the future, it makes sense to pay more attention to the intellectual tools that will be required in any future. This suggests focusing on how models of critical thought can be used differently at different times and in different situations. The idea is to put more emphasis on concepts with high generalizability—like collaborative problem solving, reflection, perceptive thinking, self-direction, and the motivation needed for life-long learning. A more thoughtful and personalized brand of learning is the goal.

Information isn't a substitute for thinking. But information and thinking are not antithetical. At higher levels, thinking requires quickly sorting through a wealth of information to be effective. There will never be enough time to teach all the information that we feel is useful. But time must be taken to be sure that student thinking can transform knowledge in a way that makes it transferable to the outside world. When there is time for inquiry and reflection, covering less can actually help students learn more deeply.

Within this context the following thinking skills can be taught directly:

- Generating multiple ideas about a topic
- Figuring out meaning from context
- Understanding analogy
- Detecting reasoning fallacies

Topical knowledge (content facts), procedural knowledge (how to study and learn), and self-knowledge are all part of critical thinking. All these thinking skills are learned through interaction with the environment, the media, peers, and the school curriculum. Some students pick it up naturally while others learn reasoning skills with difficulty.

Whether it is easy or hard for those involved, education in the twenty-first century is paying more attention to unleashing the creative thinking spirit of future innovators.

PROVIDING ACCESS TO THE THOUGHTFUL LIFE

Children can demonstrate what their reasoning ability is in a number of ways: think-out-louds, videos, performances, photo collages, stories for the newspaper, Web sites, or multimedia projects that can be shared with other students and members of the community. We are already seeing glimmers of a computer-based medium that is broadly expressive and capable of capturing many aspects of human consciousness. As the twenty-first century progresses, the whole spectrum of expression is being altered.

Communication and information technology sometimes complements and sometimes supersedes previous media. Still, the basic learning process and the essence of any curriculum will continue to involve ways of engaging students in thought that matters and sharing what they find: information/knowledge/wisdom. Wisdom gives you the power to change the shape of ideas.

By giving students the truth of others, teachers can make it possible for them to discover their own. Feeling and meaning can be turned inside out as students learn how to construct their own knowledge and absorb new learning experiences in ways that make sense to them. This extends to anticipating and exploring (from many angles) the depths that await us under the surface of things, whatever those things may be.

New technologies can stimulate *or* get in the way of thoughtful behavior; each one accelerates opportunities for change within and outside of itself. Since information now arrives so fast, it leaves little time or mental space for processing, reflecting, or thinking through implications. But no matter what we do, walking down certain high-tech paths is difficult to postpone and nearly impossible to avoid.

With the assistance of digital technology, we are living through the largest increases in expressive/thinking capacity in human history. Artificial intelligence, for example, is getting better at extending human thinking and intelligence. It can act as a supplement to human thought in areas ranging from medical problems to making suggestions about what book we may want to read. When combined with other technologies, like the Internet, the arena in which thinking resonates is vastly expanded.

There is no reason for educators to wait around hoping that someone will make the kind of instructional changes they want. A better approach is for every informed teacher and every informed citizen to push for changes in their domain of influence.

SUMMARY, CONCLUSION, AND LOOKING TO THE FUTURE

In many ways, a wide range of technology expands the traits found in our minds. We also know that every new idea or technology has unexpected consequences for thinking, but it's hard to get specific about what they are going to be. The characteristics of technology matter, but it is even more important to consider the context in which technology is used. Like people, our whiz-bang gadgets have multiple selves that emerge (or don't) based on context.

The creation of something new often goes against traditional approaches and the authority of the present. Likewise, creative and critical thinking (like innovation) are by their very nature subversive and outside the specified lines of behavior. Still, the ability to think critically and act creatively is an essential part of today's educational package.

Fostering the critical and creative imagination is one of the most important recommendations found in the new subject matter standards. Each set of content standards has its own way of suggesting how students may be helped to move beyond literal meanings to critically interpret what they read, view, or create. More than simply recording facts, "writing" with various media is viewed as a special vehicle for analyzing, interpreting, and explaining.

Education is fluid and organic. Practice is enriched by theory. Theory is transformed in the light of practice—and research plays a clarifying role in this complementary process. The standards are grounded in a framework that relies on all three. As far as creative and critical thinking is concerned, they are woven into each set of standards and therefore extend across the curriculum.

As far as instruction is concerned, it is important for teachers to tune in to what students are doing in a way that helps the teachers recognize interests and patterns of thinking so that lessons can be adjusted. Remember, thinking skills are part of a process that builds on previous experience to help us go about building knowledge and understanding (Leicester, 2010).

Learning in a socially connected world changes both *what* and *how* we think. So it is little wonder that the social side of expanding our reality (thinking) has an increasingly crucial role to play in schooling.

The future is not just something that is just going to automatically happen to us. It is something we can think about, revise, edit, and try to shape. To optimize the possibilities, our thought processes have to be flexible enough to accommodate change as new information, research, and concerns spring to life.

As new ideas come up and connections are made across subjects and everyday life, we are never finished with learning how to get things done. It is like this last line in an Octavio Paz poem: "Tomorrow we shall have to invent, once again, the reality of this world."

SUGGESTED RESOURCES

Berry, B. (2011). *Teaching 2030: What we must do for our students and our public schools.* New York: Teachers College Press.
Gardner, H. (1983). *Frames of mind.* New York: Basic Books.
Gladwell, M. (2005). *Blink: The power of thinking without thinking.* New York: Little, Brown & Co.
Jenson, E. (2005). *Teaching with the brain in mind.* Alexandria, VA: Association for Supervision and Curriculum Development.
Morozov, E. (2011). *The Net delusion: The dark side of Internet freedom.* New York: Public Affairs.

REFERENCES

Armstrong, T. (2009). *Multiple intelligences in the classroom.* 3rd ed. Alexandria, VA: Association for Supervision and Curriculum Development.
Bishop, E. (1968). *Brazil.* West Sussex, UK: Littlehampton Book Series.
Browne, M. N., and S. M. Keeley. (2009). *Asking the right questions: A guide to critical thinking.* 8th ed. Upper Saddle River, NJ: Prentice Hall.
Carr, N. (2010). *The shallows: What the Internet is doing to our brains.* New York: W. W. Norton & Co.
Dede, C., and J. Richards. (2012). *Digital platforms: Customizing classroom learning for each student.* New York: Teachers College Press.
Gardner, H. (1997). Multiple Intelligences as a parter in school improvement. *Educational Leadership* 55(1): 22–21.
Howie, D. (2011). *Teaching students thinking skills and strategies.* London: Jessica Kingsley Publishers.
Jacobs, H. Hayes (Ed.). (2004). *Getting results with curriculum mapping.* Alexandria, VA: Association for Supervision and Curriculum Development.
Jossey-Bass (Ed.). (2008). *Jossey-Bass reader on the brain and learning.* San Francisco: Jossey-Bass.
Langer, E. (1998). *The power of mindful learning.* Cambridge, MA: Da Capo.
Leicester, M. (2010). *Teaching critical thinking skills: Ideas in action.* London: Continuum International Publishing Group.
O'Toole, J., and D. Beckett. (2009). *Educational research: Creative thinking and doing.* Oxford: Oxford University Press.
Schank, R. (2011). *Teaching minds: How cognitive science can save our schools.* New York: Teachers College Press.
Tough, P. (2012). *How children succeed: Grit, curiosity, and the hidden power of character.* New York: Houghton Mifflin Harcourt.
Turkle, S. (2011). *Alone together: Why we expect more from technology and less from each other.* New York: Basic Books.
Whyte, D. (1994). *The heart aroused.* New York: Currency Doubleday.
Willis, J. (2006). *Research-based strategies to ignite student learning.* Alexandria, VA: Association for Supervision and Curriculum Development.

THREE

Collaborative Learning

A Role for Small Groups in Preparing Tomorrow's Innovators

There is much we can do alone.
But together we can do so much more. —Vygotsky

In one form or another, collaborative learning is one of the more important instructional tools to come along in the last thirty years. The idea of having students work together (in small groups) on the active construction of meaning rests on a solid base of research and practical experience. In addition, the standards projects recommend certain elements of collaborative or cooperative learning for reaching a diverse group of students.

In an interactive learning environment, students serve as learning resources for one another. Teamwork is viewed as one of the keys to accelerating students' imaginative development and academic achievement. The informal type of collaborative learning we discuss here builds on the social nature of learning and what we know about how students construct knowledge. The basic idea is to promote active learning in ways not possible with competitive or individualized learning models.

As far as preparing for innovation is concerned, it is important to recognize that it usually involves teamwork—and it usually moves along in small steps or in more risky transformational changes. Knowledge is a major innovation generator. But don't underestimate the element of chance; a random roll of the dice has a lot to do with outcomes. Since in many ways it is a new and useful method, product, and service, social networking may be viewed as a twenty-first-century example of innovation (Shih, 2011).

When it comes to collaboration and knowledge building in the classroom, the teacher organizes major parts of the curriculum around tasks, problems, and projects so that students can work together in small, mixed-ability groups. Lessons are designed with learning teams in mind so that students can combine their energies as they work toward a common goal. Positive interdependence amplifies student interaction by encouraging individuals to promote one another's productivity.

Whether formal or informal, collaborative learning is a proven way to make sure that all students are involved in learning the subject being studied. Along the road to academic achievement, student interaction can be improved by having group members reflect on how well they are functioning and thinking of ways to improve group work.

Here, collaborative learning is viewed as an educational approach that encourages students at various skill levels to work together, in small groups, to reach common goals. The basic idea is to move students from working alone to working in learning groups where they take responsibility for themselves and other group members.

Although the group "sinks or swims" together, individuals are held accountable because students receive information and feedback from peers and from their teacher. As you can see, we suggest borrowing ideas from collaborative learning, cooperative learning, and related research on group processes.

It is our view that by cooperating on academic tasks, students move toward becoming a community of learners, working together to enhance everyone's knowledge, proficiency, and enjoyment.

COLLABORATION AS AN APPROACH TO LEARNING

Collaborative learning might be viewed as both a personal teaching philosophy and a classroom technique. In the collaborative classroom, there is respect for individual group members' abilities and contributions.

Group responsibility and individual accountability are key factors. There is also a sharing of authority and acceptance of responsibility among group members for the group's actions. The group's results are based on consensus-building cooperation among group members.

Practitioners who build their own version of collaborative learning in the classroom sometimes view it as a way of living with and communicating with other people. The collaborative learning model sometimes allows students some say in forming friendships and interest groups. We often have the students turn in a confidential list of the four people with whom they would most like to work. But we make the final choices.

The content standards in mathematics, science, language arts, and other subjects recommend having students collaborate as they go about doing some of their schoolwork. In addition, student talk is stressed as a way for working things out among group members (National Research Council, 1996). What's missing from the standards are specific activities and organizational techniques for making collaborative groups work in the classroom.

Collaborative learning builds on what teachers know about how students construct knowledge, promoting active learning in a way not possible with competitive or with individualized learning. In a cooperative classroom, the teacher organizes major parts of the curriculum around tasks, problems, and projects that students can work through in small, mixed-ability groups. Lessons can be designed around active learning teams in a way that helps students combine energies as, and reach toward, a common goal.

Social skills, like interpersonal communication, group interaction, and conflict resolution, are developed as the collaborative learning process goes along. Students soon get the idea that if someone else does well, you do well. After each lesson, the learning group examines what they did well and what they might be able to do better (social processing). Many curriculum programs are using collaborative learning without labeling or making an issue of it; small-group work is simply viewed as part of a well-planned curriculum.

For decades, research has suggested that collaborative learning has positive effects (Slavin, 1990). A selection of findings:

- *Collaborative learning can motivate students who are having difficulties with math and science.* Students talk and work together on a project or problem and experience the fun of sharing ideas and information.
- Classroom interaction with others causes students to make significant learning gains compared to students in traditional settings.
- *It may help encourage active listening for disinterested students.* Students learn more when they are actively engaged in discovery and problem solving. Collaboration sparks an alertness of mind not achieved in passive listening.
- *Collaboration may help students with literacy and language skills.* Group work offers students many opportunities to use and improve speaking skills. This is particularly important for second-language learners.
- *It often provides greater psychological health for frustrated learners.* Collaborative learning gives students a sense of self-esteem, builds self-identity, and aids in their ability to cope with stress and adversity. It links individuals to group success, so that students are supported, encouraged, and held responsible individually and collectively.
- *Collaboration can help prepare students for today's society.* Team approaches to solving problems, combining energies with others, and

working to get along are valued skills in the world of work, community, and leisure.

- *Collaborative learning frequently increases respect for diversity.* Students who work together in mixed-ability groups are more likely to select mixed racial and ethnic friendships. When students cooperate to reach a common goal, they learn to appreciate and respect one another, from those who are physically handicapped to those who are mentally and physically gifted.
- *It can improve teacher effectiveness with all learners.* By actively engaging students in the learning process, teachers also make important discoveries about their students' learning. As students take some of the teaching responsibilities, the power of the teacher can be multiplied (Snodgrass and Bevevino, 2000).

SOCIAL NETWORKS AND UNDERAGE USERS

We all know about young adults and their enthusiasm for social networks. But there are a surprising number of children using sites like Facebook and MySpace. In one grade 4 class we visited, nearly half the children were familiar with Facebook, even though there is little on the site that is intended for children. (On the surface, games and digital socializing were prime attractions.)

Social networking sites realize that they have a problem and try to protect youngsters from predators. Still, there is general agreement that verifying age over the Internet is someplace between difficult and impossible. Social networking sites generally require users to be thirteen or older, but age inflation is common (eighteen is the magic number for some activities).

Students need to realize that unflattering information, images, comments they post on Google, Facebook, Twitter, LinkedIn, and other social networking sites are hard to erase. Flickr photos and personal items placed on Wikipedia can be edited and moved around by anyone. So it should be clear that callous oversharing is a threat to privacy and reputation—as well as future personal, school, and job prospects. Of course, it is technically possible to remove unwanted items, but it is difficult and one can never be completely sure of having gotten everything.

The fact that the Internet can be a vehicle for damaging someone's life online has serious implications for life off-line. Whatever the required age, children and young adults who pretend to be older can bypass safeguards. And there seems to be little anyone can do about it. In one sense, it's a little like other imaginative technologies in that social media can subvert and disrupt traditional arrangements.

The good news is that many of the parents we interviewed said their youngsters carefully monitored and used social networks responsibly. It is important to note that those parents who were involved in their children's online activities had the most positive views of the results. Whatever the reality, it is especially hard to keep young adults out of social media. In fact, one parent told us that she would rather let her child join Facebook in the open than have him go behind her back.

SOME SUGGESTIONS FOR ARRANGING THE COLLABORATIVE CLASSROOM

In schools across the country, teachers are spending less time in front of the class and more time encouraging students to work together in small groups. Straight rows are giving way to pods of three, four, or five desks. Of course, collaborative learning is more than rearranging desks. It involves changing how students interact with one another and designing lessons so that teamwork is required to complete assigned tasks.

In the collaborative classroom, group learning tasks are based on shared goals and outcomes. Teachers structure lessons so that to complete a project or activity, individuals have to work together to accomplish group goals. At the same time, teachers help students learn teamwork skills like staying with the group, encouraging participation, elaborating on ideas, and providing critical analysis.

One of the keys to success is building a sense of cooperation in the classroom. Teachers often start by providing the class with a collaborative activity. The second step is to have groups of three or four students work together on an initial exploration of ideas and information. To encourage group interdependence, teachers can use a small group version of a strategy like K-W-H-L-S.

- What do we *know*?
- What do we *want to learn*?
- *How will I work with others to learn it*?
- What have I *learned*?
- How have I *shared* what I learned from others?

We suggest that teachers give time for individual and group reflection in the last phase of any collaborative learning activity. This way, struggling learners can analyze what they have learned and identify strengths and weaknesses in the group learning process. Questions like "tell something that would help us work better next time" and "how did you contribute to the quality of the group work" also help in this social processing stage. Teachers might go on to have student groups engage in activities to reshape their knowledge or information by organizing, clarifying, and elaborating on what has been learned. It's often a good idea to ask student groups to present their findings before an interested and critical audience.

Besides encouraging a sense of group purpose, teachers need to help each student feel that he or she can contribute actively and effectively to class activities. The group may sink or swim together, but individuals are still held accountable for understanding the material. In the collaborative classroom, teachers do more than set standards for group work. They use various assessment tools to evaluate group projects, assignments, and teamwork skills. To get at individual accountability, consider randomly quizzing group members after group work is completed. Whether or not you decide to interrupt the group is one thing, but providing for some form of individual assessment is a basic requirement.

COLLABORATIVE LEARNING IN THE INTEGRATED EDUCATION CLASSROOM

Collaborative learning has been cited as an instructional strategy that can connect a wide range of struggling students to the regular classroom routines (Slavin, 1990). It has become popular because of its potential for motivating and academically engaging all students within a social setting.

It is difficult to arrange educational policy around a single policy— especially one that may change with the political winds. We suggest that a variety of approaches and a wide range of educational research are needed to determine what works best in certain situations.

Mounting evidence suggests that integrated applications and collaboration can provide positive outcomes for all students (Gillies, Ashman, and Terwel, 2008). It requires the combined talents of the regular classroom teacher and those of the special educator as well as the related service providers.

THE ADVANTAGES OF COLLABORATIVE LEARNING

Understanding the important role that collaboration plays in the process of integrated education provides a way to look at the benefits of collaboration.

1. Each person brings experiences to the collaborative process that are shared with others.
2. Support is provided for the classroom teacher.
3. Realistic expectations are determined.
4. Classroom teachers are given support for making modifications.
5. Students can be successful when appropriate modifications are made.

6. Teachers become part of a team in dealing with learning and behavior problems.

It is frequently the case that when a student with disabilities is included in the regular classroom, the assumption is made that he or she is there for academic reasons. The reality is that he or she is there to learn. The regular classroom provides a wealth of opportunities for learning.

APPLYING THE POWER OF COLLABORATIVE LEARNING

By engaging students in the process of making sense of what they are studying, children have more power to explore freely and to meaningfully connect to the subject. In a collaborative environment, the teacher assists children in the construction of meaning and acts more like a facilitator and less like a transmitter of knowledge. When questions that connect to student experience are raised collectively, ideas and strengths can be shared in a manner that supports the cooperative search for understanding.

A supportive team structure leads to greater productivity for all students. To be successful, each child needs to be held responsible for doing a fair share of the group work. At their best, cooperative groups go beyond individual learning to promote an informal style of question asking, critical thinking, and action plans for all students. Critical analysis and creative problem solving are a natural part of this active learning process.

Some common characteristics of collaborative groups are that the small group of students shares learning tasks and outcomes, and positive group collaboration is developed by setting mutual goals by the teacher and the students. When this is achieved, there is a group task commitment and individual accountability.

Group learning thrives in an atmosphere of mutual helpfulness where students know what's happening—and why. Part of creating the right environment means having the *teacher* define objectives, talk about the benefits of collaborative learning, and explain expectations and behaviors such as brainstorming, peer teaching, and confidence building.

PROMOTING ACTIVE LEARNING

Whether it is applied to finding out about new concepts, solving problems, or questioning factual information, a collaborative approach has been shown to develop academic skills. At the same time, it taps students' self-esteem and builds students' understanding and attitudes about the subject. Working together to accomplish shared goals is the key to collaborative learning. Academic success, future employment, and even everyday life demand the ability to sort through information, educate others, make sound judgments, and work as a team. Learning to work with others, persevering, solving problems, and dealing collectively with an innovation-based world are all part of the challenges facing today's students.

Struggling learners often face a difficult challenge in trying to keep up with today's classroom activities. The key to assisting students is to identify who is going to have trouble early on and provide a number of ways for students who are at risk to receive support. For example, early intervention programs can provide intensive support at the onset of a child's school career. There is growing evidence that such programs can also prevent problems from occurring in later years (Jung and Guskey, 2011).

COLLABORATION AND HUMAN BEHAVIOR

Cooperation is a major factor that differentiates humans from most other species. In addition, small-group human collaboration sets up the infrastructure that allows for all sorts of transformational changes. From complicated language patterns to complex technology, teamwork makes all the difference in the world (Tomasello, 2009). Individuals can't, for example, build a large airplane alone; it takes thousands of people cooperating to get the job done.

In most other species, only related individuals help one another. In humans, it is more broadly based and the larger social network can develop knowledge and innovations more easily. In fact, many assume that a shift in social behavior was a key factor in making humans unique (Chapais, 2008).

TEAMWORK SKILLS

No matter how you view collaborative student teamwork, there are many common principles. Instruction is not viewed as something that isolated students should have done to them; learning is something done best in association with others. The social context matters. And the way different communications are authored or coauthored affects the understanding, reception, and production of information and knowledge.

Teamwork skills do not develop automatically. They must be taught. As group members work together to produce joint work projects, teachers need to quietly help students having problems promote one another's success through sharing, explaining, and encouraging. Teachers may not be on center stage all the time, but with collaborative learning they constantly guide, challenge, and encourage students. They can also help build supportive group environments by explaining collaborative procedures to students, monitoring small-group questions, and helping students assess group effectiveness at the end of an activity.

Crafting group work that supports learning for all students requires content and activities that support cohesive small groups and meet the needs of individuals. Some teachers use some form of collaborative learning in pairs or groups of three or four students about half the time. Others may set aside less time for cooperative group work. However you set it up, collaborative learning can help your students move beyond competitive and individualistic goal structures.

As individuals within a group come to care about one another, they become more inclined to provide each other with academic assistance and personal support. They are also more likely to make suggestions for what might be done to improve group efforts in the future. As each person adds his or her unique spirit, the cooperative group takes on enough power to illuminate the consequences of alternative courses of action. It sometimes takes a little time to get cooperative groups up to speed, but it's worth the effort.

MAKING COLLABORATIVE LEARNING WORK

Like anything else, the ability of the teacher is the key to successfully using collaborative learning. By arousing interest and broadening horizons, teachers can amplify the joy and curiosity that are natural parts of the teaching and learning process. For these things to happen, teachers must be masters of content and equally familiar with the characteristics of effective interactive instruction.

Getting collaborative learning to work for you requires more than giving well-meaning instructions to "work together" and "be a team." Not all groups are collaborative. To structure lessons so that students do work collaboratively with one another requires an understanding of what makes collaboration work.

An important part of collaboration is structuring an environment where group members understand they are connected with one another in a way that one student cannot succeed unless everyone succeeds (*your success benefits me and my success benefits you*). Group goals and tasks must be designed and carefully communicated so that students believe they share a common fate (*we all sink or swim together in this class*). When the team is solidly structured, it tells students that each member has a unique contribution to make to the joint effort (*we cannot do it without you*).This creates a commitment to the success of the group as well as the individual student. No group member has all the information or all the skills. Even the least able student can recognize this.

Teaching Suggestions for Using Collaborative Learning

- Use your existing lessons, content, and curricula, and structure them in cooperative groups.
- Take any lesson in any subject area with a student of any age and structure it collaboratively.
- Tailor collaborative learning lessons to your unique instructional needs. This may mean that you may need to allow for additional time for planning.
- Diagnose the problems some students may have in working together and intervene to increase the effectiveness of the group process.
- Teach students the skills they need to work in groups. Social skills do not magically appear when collaborative lessons are employed. Skills such as "use quiet voices," "stay with your group," "take turns," and "use each other's names" are the beginning collaborative skills.
- It is important to have students discuss how well their group is doing. Groups should describe what worked well and what was harmful in their team efforts. Continuous improvement of the collaborative learning process results from careful analysis of how members are working together.

ARRANGING THE CLASSROOM FOR COLLABORATIVE LEARNING

Effective teachers know that an important step in changing student interaction is changing the seating arrangement. Architecture and the organization of our public and private spaces strongly influence our lives at every level. The same principle applies to schools and individual classrooms. The way teachers arrange classroom space and furniture has a strong impact on how students learn. When desks are grouped in a small circle or square, or when students sit side by side in pairs, collaborative possibilities occur naturally. Straight rows send a very different message.

A classroom designed for student interaction makes just about anything more interesting. The way you design the interior space of your classroom helps focus visual attention. It also sets up acoustic expectations and can help control noise levels. Natural lighting, carpets, comfortable corners, occasional music, and computers that are arranged for face-to-face interaction can all help set the general feelings of well-being, enjoyment, and morale. Classroom management is actually easier if students know that they can't shout across the classroom but they can speak quietly to one, two, or three others depending on the size of the small group. Even many questions that students are used to asking the teacher can come after asking one or two peers. All students benefit in this kind of group learning situation, even the most reluctant student.

As students engage in collaborative learning, they should sit in a face-to-face learning group that is as close together as possible. The more space you can put between groups, the better. From time to time, it is important to remix the groups so that everybody gets the chance to work with a variety of class members. The physical arrangement should allow you to speak to the whole class without too much student movement. Struggling students benefit from this grouping arrangement. Teachers can give students more of their attention and better differentiate instruction. When the whole class is together, you should be able make eye contact with every student in every group without anyone getting bent out of shape or moving desks (Joiner, Miell, Faulkner, and Littleton, 2000).

WAYS TEACHERS CAN ORGANIZE FOR COLLABORATIVE LEARNING

1. *Formulate objectives.*

   Decide on the size of groups, arrange the room, and distribute the materials students need.
2. *Explain the activity and the collaborative group structure.*
3. *Describe the behaviors you expect to see during the lesson.*

   Group behaviors:

   - Share ideas
   - Respect others
   - Ask questions
   - Stay in your group
   - Give encouragement
   - Stay on task
   - Use quiet voices

4. *Assign roles.*

   Classes new to the collaborative approach sometimes assign each member of the group a specific function that will help the group complete the assigned task. For example: the *reader* reads the problem, the *checker* makes sure that it is understood, the *animator* keeps it interesting and on task, and the *recorder* keeps track of the group work and tells the whole class about it. If you have groups of three, then everyone can share the animator's role. Struggling learners need to be included in these roles. No matter how you set up collaborative learning, group achievement depends on how well the group does *and* how well individuals within the group learn.
5. *Monitor or intervene when needed.*

While you conduct the lesson, check on each learning group when needed to improve the task and teamwork. Bring closure to the lesson.

6. *Evaluate the quality of student work.*

Ensure that students themselves will evaluate the effectiveness of their learning groups. Have students construct a plan for improvement. Be sure that all students are on task. Groups may be evaluated based on how well members performed as a *group*. The group can also give individuals specific information about their contribution. Groups can keep track of who explains concepts, encourages participation, checks for understanding, and helps organize the work (Johnson and Johnson, 2000).

Learning with a small circle of friends can help students navigate the untidy clutter of doubt and strive for things that had previously exceeded their grasp. Working in a community with others is the best way for struggling students to gain the confidence and the power to see what can be, that isn't yet.

PROBLEM SOLVING IN A SOCIAL SETTING

Problem solving and collaboration are common themes that cut across the content standards and the curriculum. But learning to solve problems in school is often different from the way it happens outside school. When they get out in the real world, students may feel lost because nobody's telling them what to solve. In real life, we are usually not confronted with a clearly stated problem with a simple solution. Often, we have to work with others to just figure out what the problem is. The same thing is true when it comes to asking and answering questions. When teachers and students can relate to other people, it can bring out the best in them and in others.

Knowledge is constructed over time by learners within a meaningful social setting. Students talking and working together on a project or problem experience the fun and the joy of sharing ideas and information. When students construct knowledge together, they have opportunities to compare knowledge, talk it over with peers, ask questions, justify their position, confer, and arrive at a consensus. Even students who usually struggle with a project will feel a sense of belonging to the group.

Collaboration will not occur in a classroom that requires students to always raise their hands to speak. Active listening is not sitting quietly as a teacher or another student drones on. It requires spontaneous and polite interruptions where everyone has an equal chance to speak and interact. Just let others complete a thought and don't break into the conversation in midsentence. Try to get everyone to ask a question or make a comment. It may be best not to make students put their hand up first. Encourage the more talkative class members to let everyone make a contribution before they make another point. The inattentive listener may need to assume a leadership role and help monitor the discussion.

Collaborative learning will involve some change in the noise level of the classroom. Sharing and working together even in controlled environments will be louder than an environment where students work silently from textbooks. With experience, teachers learn to keep the noise constructive. Whether you are a parent or a teacher, you know that a little reasoning (regarding rules) won't hurt children. Responsible behavior needs to be developed and encouraged with consistent classroom patterns.

When collaborative problem solving is over, students need to spend time reflecting on the group work. This can be sparked by a basic question at the end: "What worked well and how might the process be improved?" Students and teachers need to be involved in evaluating learning products and the collaborative group environment.

Effective interpersonal skills are not just for a collaborative learning activity; they also benefit students in later educational pursuits and when they enter the workforce. Social interactions are fundamental to negotiating meaning and building a personal rendition of knowledge. Mixed-ability learning groups have proven effective across the curriculum. It is important to involve students in establishing rules for active group work.

CLASS RULES FOR COLLABORATIVE LEARNING

Rules should be kept simple and might include the following:

- Everyone is responsible for his or her work.
- Productive talk is desired.
- Each person is responsible for his or her own behavior.
- Try to learn from others within your small group.
- Everyone must be willing to help anyone who asks.
- Ask the teacher for help if no one in the group can answer the question.

Group roles and individual responsibilities also need to be clearly defined and arranged so that each group member's contribution is unique and essential. If the learning activities require materials, students may be required to take responsibility for assembling and storing them. Avoid getting too many materials too fast. Three or four problems with materials are enough for the struggling learner. All students want to be using materials. Unlike competitive learning situations, the operative pronoun in collaborative learning is "we," not "me."

TEACHING THE COLLABORATIVE GROUP LESSON

During the initial introduction of a lesson, you can help your students understand what it is they're supposed to do by establishing guidelines on how the group work needs to be conducted. Present and review the necessary concepts or skills with the whole class and pose a part of the problem or an example of a problem for the whole class to try. Provide a lot of opportunities for your students to discuss a wide range of issues that are meaningful to them. Present the actual group problem after you finish the conceptual overview. Then, encourage them to discuss and clarify the problem task.

When they're ready, students start to work collaboratively to solve problems. You'll need to listen to the ideas of the different teams and offer assistance when you detect that some of them are getting stuck. You're also responsible for designing extension activities in case the faster teams finish early. There are different ways of handling teams that are stuck. One way would be for you to help them discover what they know so far and then pose a simple example or, perhaps, point out a misconception or erroneous idea that may be getting in their way.

For example, team members may have trouble getting along with one another or focusing on the one very specific task they're supposed to be doing. Pull their energies together by asking them simple questions such as, "What are you supposed to be doing now?" "What is your team's task?" "How will you get organized from where you are now?" "What materials do you need?" "Do you think you have enough time to cover everything you set out to do?" "Do you know who will do what?" This is very helpful for disengaged students.

After students complete the problem task and group exploration stages, they will need to meet again as a whole class to summarize and present their findings. All the teams need to present their solutions and tell their classmates how they worked toward their resolution as a group.

You or the other students in class could very well ask questions such as, "How did you organize the task?" "What problems did your team have?" "What method did you use?" "Was your group method effective? Why or why not?" "Did anyone have a different method or strategy for solving the same or a similar problem?" "Did your team think that your solution made sense?"

Encourage your students to listen and respond to their classmates' comments. You may, in fact, point out to them that they could earn participation points in this exercise by responding precisely to their classmates' remarks and building on them. Ask the recorder in the group to make notes on the chalkboard and write down students' responses to help summarize class data at the end of the lesson.

HELPING ALL LEARNERS SUCCEED

This section introduces classroom strategies for helping all students succeed in a regular classroom setting. Ten suggestions are offered from a variety of research studies from "Strategies for Helping At-Risk Students" to "Alternative Approaches in Planning for Academic Content."

A collaborative group structure allows for high levels of flexibility and creativity. One approach that has promise is the use of flexible grouping strategies essential in collaborative learning, which according to a number of studies, improves everything from achievement to self-esteem (Slavin, 1990). Here we describe a flexible grouping strategy that can be used with students of all ability levels.

1. Assign students to flexible groups.

Organize the class into groups of four. One way to accomplish this is to use partner groups. Rank the class from the "most prepared" to the "least prepared" for the subject (e.g., number the students from 1 to 30). Next, divide them into subgroups (1 to 10, 11 to 20, 21 to 30) so that the groups are similar to the traditional high, middle, and low ability groups. Finally, achieve mixed grouping by assigning the top student in each of the three groups to one group, the second-highest student in each to another, the third-highest student to another, and so on. You will then have students 1, 11, students 10, 20, and 30. In this way, the mixed groups should comprise students who are sufficiently different in ability that they can benefit from one another's help, but not so different that they find one another intimidating.

Inform students of their group assignments, and tell them that they are partners and must help one another as needed, whether by reading one another's work before it is turned in, by answering questions regarding assignments, by showing a partner how to do something, or by discussing a story and sharing their ideas. Let them know that this is only one of many grouping arrangements that you will be using. Grouping procedures may be based on skills, levels, or interests. Collaborative groups can be based on tasks or goal achievement.

2. Focus on the needs of students.

Students learn best when they satisfy their own motives for learning the material. Some of these motivations include the need to learn something in order to complete a particular task or activity, the need for new experiences, and the need to be involved and to interact with other people (Yard and Vatterott, 1995).

3. Make students active participants in learning.

Students learn by doing, making things, writing, designing, creating, and solving problems. The first step is to honor the different ways that students learn.

4. Help students set achievable goals for themselves.

Students often fail to meet unrealistic goals. Encourage students who are struggling to focus on their continued improvement. Help students evaluate their progress by having them critically look at their work and the work of their peers.

5. Work from students' strengths and interests.

Teachers may give students interest inventories to help them find areas where they have a special talent or interest, such as sports, art, or car mechanics. Ultimately, each student selects an area of special interest or curiosity and discusses the topic with the teacher and his or her peers. Then, they begin a search for more information, which may lead to a group project or a team presentation (Tomlinson and Edison, 2003).

6. Be aware of the problems students are having.

Meet with your students one-on-one for a brief conference. It's helpful to record the conversation so you have an oral explanation of their understandings. Play the recording for your student and ask questions if the student is confused.

7. Organize a conducive team-meeting environment.

Students often are easily distracted by the sights and sounds in the room. Choose an area of the classroom that presents the fewest distractions and keep visual displays purposeful.

8. Incorporate more time and practice for students.

Students who are having difficulties remembering skills need small doses of increased practice throughout the day. This increases performance.

9. Provide clarity.

Clarity is achieved by modeling and using open-ended questions so you can adjust your approach to different students.

10. Intervene early and often.

The key to intervention strategies is identifying students who need extra help and providing ways for struggling students to receive support.

COLLABORATIVE LEARNING ACTIVITIES

A carefully balanced combination of integrated education, subject matter knowledge, knowledge of the students, instruction, self-monitoring, and active group work help meet diverse needs of all students. The activities suggested here are designed to provide a collaborative vehicle for active learning in math and science.

Activity 1: Build a Square

This activity can be used with just about any elementary or middle school class. It relates to the geometry standard in math and the communication standard in both math and science.

Materials

An envelope containing five puzzle pieces. Either the teacher or the students can make the puzzle pieces from three-inch squares of index cards. Cut the index cards into three pieces. Place the puzzle pieces in an envelope.

Procedures

Five people around your table will all make an individual square. Each square has three pieces. Each group leader opens the envelope and passes out the puzzle pieces like a deck of cards so each person has three pieces. *No one is allowed to talk or gesture during this activity.* Group members can pick up a piece and offer it to someone in their group. They can take it or refuse it. *No reaching over and taking pieces!* Raise your hands when all the exchanges have been made and all five squares are completed. Students work together silently. They are eagerly trying to get their squares done. It is almost impossible for a struggling student to fail when the whole group is focused.

Evaluation

Next, try the activity again, only this time everyone is allowed to talk.

Take time to have a class discussion concerning the problems each group had. Suggest ideas that would make this activity work better.

Activity 2: Back-to-Back Communication

This can be used from grade 3 through middle school. It relates to the geometry and measurement standards in math and the communication standard in both math and science.

Materials

Cut out shapes that can be easily moved on a desk. Make many geometric shapes and make each shape a different color. Colored paper is the simplest material, but Attribute Blocks or Pattern Blocks can also be used.

Procedures

1. Give each group of two people two envelopes with matching sets of shapes. Students at a beginning level should get five or six shapes. More advanced students might use a dozen or more.
2. Have children get into groups of two, seated back-to-back, with their envelopes in front of them.

3. Tell students one of them is the teller and the other listens and tries to follow directions exactly.
4. The teller arranges one shape at a time in a pattern. As the teller does this, he or she gives the listener exact directions: what the shape is and where to place it.
5. When the pattern is finished, have students check how well they have done.
6. Switch roles and do it again.

Evaluation

Have students explain the activity to a partner and describe what was difficult, and how they did it.

Activity 3: Investigate Your Time Line

This works from grade 3 through middle school. Among other things, it relates to the measurement standard in mathematics.

Objectives

1. Working in groups of four or five, each group makes a time line of the ages of the people in their groups and the events in their lives.
2. Students will compare the events in their lives with those of other students. (For example: "the most important event for me when I was five years old was. . . ").
3. Students record and report the results.

Background Information

- A time line can show different cultural and ethnic patterns.
- Students are able to see how maturity affects decisions.
- A time line exercise is designed to find out how time changes students' math and science perceptions.

Materials

A thirteen-foot-long piece of butcher paper for each group, rulers, fine-point markers, and a time line prepared by the teacher to post on the board for the students to use as a model.

Procedures

1. The teacher will explain that the students will be working in collaborative groups to make time lines of the ages and lives of the people in their groups.

2. The teacher will divide students into groups of four or five.
3. The teacher and students will pass out the materials to each group.
4. The teacher will explain his or her model time line and give students directions for making their own time lines:

- Students will find out the ages of the people in their group: who is the oldest, next oldest, youngest, and so on.
- Students will start the time line on January 1 of the year that the oldest person in the group was born.
- Students will end the time line on the last day of the current year.
- Each student will use a different color marker to mark off each year.
- Each year equals one foot, and an inch equals a month.
- At the bottom of each year, the students will write the important events in their lives.
- A color key with the colors of markers and each student's name will identify the student. Students can put a dot or star by the important events in their lives such as birthdays, births of siblings, and other important events in their lives.

Evaluation

A volunteer from each group will present the group's time line and post it on the classroom bulletin board.

Activity 4: Bridge Building

This is intended for grades 3 through 9. It supports the measurement, geometry, and communication standards in math and the physical science, investigation, and experiment standards in science. Bridge Building is an interdisciplinary math and science activity that reinforces skills related to communication, group process, social studies, language arts, technology, and the arts.

Materials

Lots of newspaper, masking tape, one large heavy rock, and one cardboard box. Have students bring in stacks of newspaper. You will need approximately a one-foot pile of newspapers per small group.

Procedures

1. For the first part of this activity, divide students into groups of about four. Each group will be responsible for investigating one aspect of bridge building.

Group 1: Research

This group is responsible for going to the library and looking up facts about bridges, collecting pictures of all kinds of bridges, and bringing back information to be shared with the class.

Group 2: Aesthetics, Art, Literature

This group must discover songs, books, paintings, artwork, and so on, which deal with bridges.

Group 3: Measurement, Engineering

This group must discover design techniques, blueprints, angles, and measurements of actual bridge designs. If possible, visit a local bridge to look at the structural design and other features.

Have the group representatives get together to present their findings to the class. Allow time for questions and discussion. The second part of this activity involves actual bridge construction with newspapers and masking tape.

1. Assemble the collected stacks of newspaper, tape, the rock, and the box at the front of the room. Divide the class into groups. Each group is instructed to take a newspaper pile and several rolls of masking tape. Explain that the group will be responsible for building a stand-alone bridge using only the newspapers and tape. The bridge is to be constructed so that it can support the large rock and so that the box can pass underneath.

2. Planning is crucial. Each group is given ten minutes of planning time in which they are allowed to talk and plan together. During the planning time they are not allowed to touch the newspapers and tape, but they are encouraged to pick up the rock and make estimates of how high the box is, make a sketch of the bridge, or assign group roles of responsibility.

3. At the end of the planning time, students are given about fifteen minutes to build their bridge. During this time, there is no talking among the group members. They may not handle the rock or the box—only the newspapers and tape. A few more minutes may be necessary to ensure that all groups have a chance to get their constructions to meet at least one of the two "tests" (rock or box). If a group finishes early, its members can add some artistic flourishes to their bridge or watch the building process in other groups. (With children, you may not want to stop the process until each group can pass at least one "test.")

Evaluation

Stop all groups at the allotted time. Survey the bridges with the class and allow each group to try to pass the two tests for their bridge. They get to pick which test is first. Does the bridge support the rock? Does the box fit underneath? Discuss the design of each bridge and how they compare to the bridges researched earlier. Try taking some pictures of the completed bridges before you break them down and put them in a recycling bin. Awards could be given for the most creative bridge design; the sturdiest, the tallest, and the widest bridge; the best group collaboration; and so on. Remember, each group is proud of its bridge.

PROBLEM SOLVING IN COLLABORATIVE CLASSROOMS

In a classroom that values teamwork, teachers provide time for students to grapple with problems, try out strategies, discuss issues, experiment, explore, and evaluate. A key element in collaborative classrooms is group interdependence. This means that the success of each individual depends on the success of each of the other group members.

Student investigations, team discussions, and group projects go hand in hand with preparing students for the new information, knowledge, and work arrangements that they will encounter throughout life. Also, partner teams can work as well as teams of three or four—and better than groups of five or six (Bishop and Allen-Malley, 2004).

Data is a valuable resource and information a valuable commodity, but teamwork is the key to making imaginative things happen. Whatever variation of collaborative inquiry a teacher chooses, students can be given opportunities to integrate their learning through interactive discovery experiences and applying their problem-solving skills.

Activity

Form groups of two, three, or four, and come up with captions for pictures or political cartoons from the newspaper. An alternative is to come up with the caption and search for a cartoon or picture that works with it. Students can look for something that relates to whatever topic they are studying. Share with the class.

Across all subjects it is more important to emphasize the *reasoning* involved in working on a problem than it is getting the "answer." Near the end of a group project, the teacher can develop more class unity by pointing out how each small group's research effort contributes to the class goal of understanding and exploring a topic.

Teachers need to model attitudes and present themselves as collaborative problem solvers and models of learning. They do this by letting students know that learning is a lifelong process for teachers and other adults. A suggestion: let them in on some of your more positive professional development experiences.

ATTITUDES CHANGE AS CHILDREN COLLABORATE

Some students may require a shift in values and attitudes if a collaborative learning environment is to succeed. The traditional school experience has taught many students that the teacher is there to validate their thinking and direct learning. Getting over years of learned helplessness may take time.

Attitudes change as students learn to work cooperatively. As they share rather than compete for recognition, struggling students find time for reflection and assessment. Small groups can write collective stories, edit one another's writing, solve problems, correct homework, prepare for tests, investigate questions, examine artifacts, work on a computer simulation, brainstorm an invention, create a sculpture, or arrange music. Working together is also a good way for students to synthesize what they have learned, collaboratively present to a small group, coauthor a written summary, or communicate concepts.

It is important that students understand that simply "telling an answer" or "doing someone's work" is not helping a classmate learn. Helping involves learning to ask the right question to help someone grasp the meaning or explaining with an example. These understandings need to be actively and clearly explained, demonstrated, and developed by the teacher.

A major benefit of collaborative inquiry is that students are provided with group stimulation and support. The small group provides safe opportunities for trial and error as well as a safe environment for asking questions or expressing opinions. More students get chances to respond, raise ideas, or ask questions. As each student brings unique strengths and experiences to the group and contributes to the group process, respect for individual differences is enhanced.

The group also acts as a motivator. We all feel a little nudge when we participate in group activities. Many times, ideas are pushed beyond what an individual would attempt or suggest on his or her own. Group interaction enhances idea development, and students have many leadership skills when they become teachers as well as learners. In addition, the small-group structure extends children's resources as they are encouraged to pool strategies and share information.

If the group is small enough, it's hard for the more withdrawn students not to participate. Students soon learn that they are capable of validating their own values and ideas. This frees teachers to move about, work with small groups, and interact in a more personal manner with students.

SKILLFUL COLLABORATION AMPLIFIES LEARNING AND INNOVATION

If one person's achievement in a group is viewed as another's loss, then cooperation, openness, and generosity fade and self-interest and fear move front and center. Collaborative learning is designed to emphasize the positive and stimulate the best that everyone has to offer. It has proven itself as an effective way to provide peer support for imaginative behavior in the classroom.

Collaborative group problem solving, reciprocal teaching, and cross-age tutoring are now generally accepted as useful tools for helping students get the most out of any subject. As technology charms us with its quick and easy attractions, brain functions can get lazy and encourage people to take the easy way out. The brain needs substantial face-to-face off-line exercise to operate at its collaborative best (Brown and Fenske, 2010).

By collaboratively exploring new concepts in different contexts, students can internalize mental images, perform actions, and discover underlying concepts. To gain and share expertise, team members challenge one another's thinking in a way that doesn't breed conformity or hostility. Work teams can also be used to provide struggling students with a support network that can gradually be withdrawn as children move to higher levels of confidence.

In the collaborative classroom, mutual achievement and caring can result in learning's actually becoming more personalized. Students and teachers can come to view one another as a learning community of collaborators who help group members with cognitive, emotional, physical, and social changes.

Adapting to today's social and academic realities requires a common framework and conceptual understanding.

When it comes to successful innovation, the prerequisite skills are teamwork, vision, resources, and time. And remember, failure is an inevitable cul-de-sac on the road to success. Just try to figure out what went wrong and try not to make the same mistake twice.

LEARNING IN COMMUNITY WITH OTHERS

Knowledge is rarely constructed in isolation. At just about any age, individuals do better at building understanding when they have the help of others. In a learning community, individuals collaborate in meaning-making activities. Community members are recognized for what they know (as well as what they need to learn). To be successful, each member of the group must learn how to contribute to the overall outcome. When the class is divided into collaborative groups, helping other team members isn't cheating; it is a highly regarded approach to learning subject matter. Such collaborative group work provides the keystone for building broader learning communities.

Increasingly, educational systems set out to develop individuals who can understand the world and are capable of working with others to alter it for the better. Teamwork skills are at (or near) the top of the job skills ladder. As teachers, it is our responsibility to prepare students to enter an increasingly international world with openness, confidence, and intelligence. Much of what we do is more implicit than explicit. So, it is as important for the classroom teacher to embody and to exhibit what we value in students.

To reach group goals, each individual must contribute in some way to the outcome. The result is the development of a kind of social cohesion that stems from students' learning how to be contributing members of a learning team. Students who are struggling to learn math and science need to go beyond the lower-level basics that are often designed only to improve test scores, to experience the same high-quality education that many in affluent areas take for granted.

In addition to teamwork skills, a collaborative structure can help all students by providing group support for self-discovery, problem solving, and higher-level reasoning. One of the side benefits for teachers is that positive instructional changes are most likely to occur when there is a cooperative school climate and a peer support system in place.

YESTERDAY, TODAY, AND TOMORROW

In many ways, collaborative team learning becomes a useful instructional partner because it supports the kind of deep learning that shines toward the future. It is little wonder that in one form or another, cooperative group work has become one of the most widely used instructional innovations. In skillful hands, it can build on social interaction to unleash the full potential of our children's minds.

As students learn to accomplish shared goals, they also learn to get the most out of learning and life. In addition, as teachers who have experienced or implemented collaborative group learning will tell you, the habits of the mind and the emotions of the heart associated with successful peer collaboration can be like a breeze of fresh air in the classroom (Bellanca and Stirling, 2011).

Yesterday, today, and tomorrow: successful schools have (and will) come in many colors. But there are a few common features that cut across time and space. Culture is important—this includes family, neighborhood, country, and school. One of the educational constants is the need to create a close-knit learning community where all students and their teachers care for one another. Increasingly, new technologies are enabling students to go beyond the classroom to expand their collaboration and knowledge acquisition.

Social networks, such as Facebook, can enhance feelings of social connections among self-confident youth. But social media can have the opposite effect on many; "more connected" does not mean more invested in the lives of others. Also, connecting with friends and exchanging ideas is fine, but popularity contests are a losing proposition for everyone. For example, when you're looking at someone else's status updates, pictures, and "friend" count, it is a little like those family history (and impossibly positive) Christmas letters.

When facial expression and body language are missing, (online) context takes a vacation. It is clear that face-to-face social interaction and the group transmission of norms are as essential for learning. The same can be said for developing the perception and instinct that are a large part of the student's academic motivation and personal character (Harasim, 2012).

Student learning teams are natural partners of e-learning and distance learning. As in face-to-face collaborative learning, objectives can be structured so that individual goals are influenced by the actions of other group members (social interdependence). Virtual collaboration is increasingly used in the business world, and schools are starting to realize that geographic distance doesn't necessarily get in the way of learning.

By tapping into students' natural curiosity and creating a caring learning community, teachers can help their students learn how to use collaboration to achieve academic goals. Consistent with this is including all students in daily classroom routines and teams where group accomplishment matters.

SUMMARY AND IMPLICATIONS

Within collaborative groups, all students can build on one another's strengths to develop a sense of group solidarity and accomplishment. As learners work together, they can share alternative viewpoints, support each other's inquiry, develop critical thinking skills, and improve on their academic performance.

There are many important findings on the benefits of collaborative learning, including motivation, increased academic performance, active listening, improved language and literacy skills, and a sense of self-esteem. Another major benefit of collaborative learning is that individuals are provided with group stimulation and support.

The learning group provides safe opportunities for trial and error—as well as a safe environment for asking questions or expressing opinions. Students also get more chances to respond, raise ideas, or ask questions. Each participant brings unique strengths and experiences to the group process. Along the collaborative way, respect for individual differences is enhanced and it becomes relatively easy to draw everyone into the group work (Brooks, 2011).

When teachers build on the social nature of learning, students usually become more motivated to explore meaningful inquiry and problem solving. As students learn to cooperate and work in small mixed-ability groups, they can also take on more responsibility for themselves and helping others to learn. The basic idea is that the social nature of learning builds on the continuous interaction between perception and action.

In the twenty-first century, schools need to support and understand the process of teamwork, creativity, and innovation. Clearly, students' interest in their peers is a resource that can stimulate the learning process through group activities. New technological tools can help with developing effective groups by encouraging online interpersonal communication that connects to off-line relationships. Also, tech tools can help collaborative groups evaluate data and cut through today's information clutter (Craine and Craine, 2011).

Imaginative change begins with imaginative ideas. Virtual instruction has its place, but when it comes to helping students generate new ideas, you can't substitute technology for live teachers. In fact, there is no strong research (at the K–12 level) that online work or courses are generally as effective as face-to-face learning (U.S. Department of Education, 2009). Cutting corners is one thing, benefiting students quite another.

Whether it is online or off, the dynamism of frequent and in-depth collaboration can serve as one of the engines of educational transformation. The process includes gradually internalizing instructional concepts through interactions with peers and adults—with individual and group reflection encouraged along the way. The basic idea is to build a cooperative learning environment that allows learners to thrive in a knowledge age.

Today's students *can* succeed individually by working in collaboration with their peers. And by building on group energy and idealism, the thinking, learning, and doing processes can be pushed forward in subjects across the curriculum.

> The age of cooperation is approaching. Teachers and administrators are discovering an untapped resource for accelerating students' achievement: the students themselves. —Robert Slavin

SUGGESTED RESOURCES

Christian, B. (2011). *The most human human: What talking with computers teaches us about what it means to be alive.* New York: Doubleday.

Gleick, J. (2011). *The information: A history, a theory, a flood.* New York: Pantheon.

Jolliffe, W. (2007). *Cooperative learning in the classroom: Putting it into practice.* London: Sage.

Kahn, P. (2011). *Technological nature: Adaptation and the future of human life.* Cambridge, MA: MIT Press.

National Council of Teachers of Mathematics. (2000). *Principles and standards for school mathematics.* Reston, VA: National Council of Teachers of Mathematics.

Wolfe, B., and C. Sparkman. (2010). *Team-building activities for the digital age: Using technology to develop effective groups.* Champaign, IL: Human Kinetics.

REFERENCES

Bellanca, J., and T. Stirling. (2011). *Classrooms without borders: Using Internet projects to teach communication and collaboration.* New York: Teachers College Press.

Bishop, P., and G. Allen-Malley. (2004). *The power of two: Partner teams in action.* Westerville, OH: National Middle School Association.

Brooks, D. (2011). *The social animal: The hidden sources of love, character, and achievement.* New York: Random House.

Brown J., and M. Fenske. (2010). *The winner's brain: 8 strategies great minds use to achieve success.* Cambridge, MA: Da Capo.

Chapais, B. (2008). *Primeval kinship.* Cambridge, MA: Harvard University Press.

Craine, R., and G. Craine. (2011). *Natural learning for a connected world: Education, technology, and the human brain.* New York: Teachers College Press.

Dixon-Krauss, L. (1995). *Vygotsky in the classroom: Mediated literacy instruction and assessment.* Upper Saddle River, NJ: Pearson.

Gillies, R., A. Ashman, and J. Terwel (Eds.). (2008). *The teacher's role in implementing cooperative learning in the classroom.* New York: Springer.

Harasim, L. (2012). *Learning theory and online technologies.* New York: Routledge.

Johnson, D., R. Johnson, and E. J. Holubec. (2008). *Cooperation in the classroom, revised edition.* Edina, MN: Ineraction Book Co.

Joiner, R., D. Miell, D. Faulkner, and K. Littleton (Eds.). (2000). *Rethinking collaborative learning.* London: Free Association Books.

Jung, L. A., and T. R. Guskey. (2011). *Grading exceptional and struggling learners.* Thousand Oaks, CA: Corwin.

National Research Council. (1996). *National Science Education Standards.* Washington, DC: National Academy Press.

Shih, C. (2011). *The Facebook era: Tapping online social networks to market, sell, and innovate.* Upper Saddle River, NJ: Prentice Hall.

Slavin, R. (1990). *Cooperative learning: Theory, research, and practice.* 2nd ed. Upper Saddle River, NJ: Prentice Hall.

Snodgrass, D., and M. Bevevino. (2000). *Collaborative learning in middle and secondary schools: Applications and assessments.* Larchmont, NY: Eye on Education.

Tomasello, M. (2009). *Why we cooperate.* Cambridge, MA: MIT Press.

Tomlinson, C., and C. Cunningham Edison. (2003). *Differentiation in practice: A resource guide for differentiating curriculum.* Alexandria, VA: Assocation for Supervision and Curriculum Development.

U.S. Department of Education. (2009). *Evaluation of evidence-based practices in learning: A meta-analysis and review of online learning studies.* Washington, DC: U.S. Department of Education.

FOUR

Communication Technologies

> Information has never been in short supply, but with the advent of new technologies and media, most notably the Internet, vast and often overwhelming amounts of information now deluge individuals around the clock. . . . Those who can synthesize well for themselves will rise to the top of the pack; those whose syntheses make sense to others will become invaluable teachers, communicators, and leaders. —Bellance and Brandt

Available technologies have always been tilting the classroom scene back and forth. Whether it is in or out of the classroom, new ways of communicating and relating to information have frequently required a break from habit. When a new medium emerges, it often generates new ways of thinking and the opening of new realities. A good example can be found in today's online world where the whole world may be watching and connecting names to Facebook pictures.

The arrival of a new medium has always been exhilarating and frightening, but finally it's just part of life. A few decades into the twentieth century it was the telephone that began to be taken for granted. By the 1950s it was television. Now many children and young adults see digital devices and the Internet as a natural way to extend their information and communication reach.

It is important to recognize the fact that each new technology creates a new human environment, which leads to new ways of thinking. Emerging electronic information and communications technology can conjure new environments for critical thinking, creativity, and teamwork. When used intelligently, they can help you do all kinds of things better.

In a school setting, digital technologies can encourage analytical thinking and help students connect subjects to collaborative inquiry (Caine and Caine, 2011). But still, in some ways, the same technologies and their applications encourage uncritical users to know more and more about less and less.

As educators increasingly take an active role in the development of educational technology, there is more of a reasoned curriculum connection. And the process itself can have something of a liberating effect on the imagination of all involved. Also, new technological possibilities can encourage new habits of the mind and fresh perspectives. To get all of this right requires everyone involved to view teachers' professional development as a necessity (rather than a luxury).

Unleashing the potential of digital media requires serious thinking, research, and experimentation to make the connection between technology and the characteristics of effective instruction and educational technology. Future directions are open to question. But what is clear is that new technologies herald the arrival of a different educational configuration (West, 2012).

POWERFUL TOOLS AND UNEXPECTED POSSIBILITIES

Done wrong, activities that rely on digital technology can be sad and lonely. When done right, the same technology can help an active, meaning-centered curriculum to flourish in (and beyond) the classroom. Either way, the coming together of technologies like computers, video, satellites, and the Internet is both evolutionary and revolutionary.

Where do creative solutions come from and what sparks chains of creation? Computers and their associates are potentially powerful tools for communication, academic work, and innovation. Digital technology has the power to move literacy and learning patterns off established roads. By motivating students through the excitement of discovery, a wide assortment of technological tools can assist the imaginative spirit of inquiry and make lessons sparkle. They can even put students right out on the edge of discovery—where truth throws off its various disguises.

As human horizons shift, a sort of flexible drive and intent are required for innovation and progress. Technology can add power to what we do and help us kick against educational boundaries. The vivid images of electronic media can stimulate students as they move quickly through mountains of information, pulling out important concepts and following topics of interest.

The online process changes students' relationship to information by allowing them to personally shift the relationship of knowledge elements across time and space. Learners can follow a topic between subjects, reading something here, and viewing a video segment there. All of this changes how information is structured and how it is used. It also encourages students to take more responsibility for their own learning.

The negative side of online learning is the practice of paying partial attention. Students "no longer have time to reflect, contemplate, or make thoughtful decisions. Instead they exist in a sense of constant crisis—on alert for a new contact or a bit of exciting news or information at any moment" (Rose, 2010).

> All media as extensions of ourselves serve to provide new transforming vision and awareness. —Marshall McLuhan

Be ready for the unexpected. Things don't always go as planned. When he invented the telephone, Alexander Graham Bell thought that it would be used to listen to distant symphony concerts. Thomas Edison thought that the phonograph record would be used to send messages. Some of the best thinkers often miss the potential of their inventions. For example, physicist Heinrich Hertz was the first to generate and detect radio waves, yet he dismissed the notion that his findings might ever have any practical value. Human advances often come from what may go unnoticed or seem trivial at the time.

Anything that changes perspective—from travel to technology—can help generate new ideas. The motivation is also there because it's usually more fun to do things where the unexpected may turn up than to stick with the easily predictable. Playfulness and experimentation can often open up to creative possibilities, increasing the capacity to fashion ideas or products in a novel fashion. Creatively playing with various ideas, some of which may seem silly at the time, may result in getting lucky with one or two of them.

It is often difficult to detect the subtle happenstance and how we make room in our own lives for positive accidents to happen. Being exposed to different experiences and paying attention to what's going on in the world help by opening up all kinds of serendipitous possibilities. Training the eye to notice things goes a long way toward making unpredictable advances happen. Each new finding can open up fresh questions and possibilities—breaking the habits that get in the way of creative thinking and change. Prescription for thinking in the future: following curiosity, leaving doors open, using technological tools, and making room for good luck to happen.

THE TECHNOLOGICAL DIMENSIONS OF LEARNING IN A NEW ERA

At school the challenge is getting students to apply the same level of intensity to their schoolwork that they apply to social media and video games. Building a dynamic model of learning requires making good use of everything available. But action without vision can be a nightmare . . . and vision without action often leads nowhere. One thing is certain: new technology is bound to generate new ways of thinking, learning, and working.

The playful gleam in the eye is often an engine of progress. There are multiple tools and modes of expression that schools need to build on to promote the multitude of strengths and imaginations found in all students. Many schools are mired in unproductive routines that prevent teachers from making creative breakthroughs. Still, we should recognize that it's difficult to redesign the plane when you're the pilot and flying at 30,000 feet.

Educators are not often able to take enough time to go back to the drawing board and use good data and experience to get things right. Reflection and changing approaches take time, space, support, and opportunities for collegial professional development to make all the changes required.

Powerful forms of face-to-face learning within schools must not be neglected as we sort out the new media possibilities. Intelligent uses of electronic forms of learning have proven to be helpful in improving student learning. But when it comes to the professional development of teachers, its value is not as clear. Electronic learning can, however, make a contribution. And it is a useful supplement to the professional development tool kit.

It is difficult to unravel issues of creativity or analysis without taking into account influential media, such as computers and television. They have a tremendous impact on children. We shape them and they shape us. Some are often written about as Lady Caroline wrote about Lord Byron: "mad, bad and dangerous to know." Others see technology, such as computers and the Internet, as a particularly dangerous enemy, creating a culture of electronic Peeping Toms without a moral foundation.

To be valuable, educational technology must contribute to the improvement of education. Digital devices and their accessories should be designed to help open doors to reality and provide a setting for reflection. By making important points that might otherwise go unnoticed, these technological tools can help students refine and use knowledge more effectively. For example, computers can use mathematical rules to simulate and synthesize the lifelike behavior of cells growing and dividing. It's a very convincing way to bring the schooling process to life.

The yeast of knowledge, openness, and enterprise raises the need for a multiplicity of learning media and technological tools. Schools can teach students to recognize how technology can undermine social values, human goals, and national intention. They can also help students learn to harness these powerful tools so that they might strengthen and support the best in human endeavors. It is our belief that when the pedagogical piece is in place, technology can support and strengthen the best in student learning. This can change not only what teachers teach, but also how they go about doing it.

As new technologies and related products start to fulfill their promise, students will become active participants in knowledge construction across a variety of disciplines. We have had only a glimpse of the technological gateways to learning that will open in the twenty-first century. As state-of-the-art pedagogy is connected with state-of-the-art technological tools, the way knowledge is constructed, stored, and learned will be fundamentally altered.

THE FUTURE OF NARRATIVE IN CYBERSPACE

The idea of print as an immutable cannon may or may not be a historical illusion. One thing is for sure: the way print is being mixed electronically with other media changes things. Although the American book industry is rushing into the emerging electronic literary market, book pages made of paper won't go away. And print is here to stay. Even the doomsayers usually use books to put forward their argument that the medium is a doomed and outdated technology.

In the future will books be confined to dusty museum libraries? No, they remain an elegant, user-friendly medium. With printed books, you don't need batteries and don't have to worry about the technological platform's becoming obsolete and unusable. The major goal of any form of reading instruction will continue to be getting students to comprehend what they read.

There are at least two fairly new digital approaches to books that are finding a niche the literacy universe. One is much like an electronic version of printed books. The other approach to electronic books is interactive and visually intensive. It takes the narrative and places it in randomly accessible blocks of text, graphics, and moving video. With some e-book stories, students must learn to go beyond merely following the action of the plot to learn about characters, explore different ideas, and enter other minds.

An interactive e-book story places students in charge of how things develop and how they turn out. Participants are able to change the sequence or make up a new beginning to a multidimensional story. They can slow down to find out additional information and they can change the ending. Navigating interactive stories with no fixed center, beginning, or end can be very disconcerting to the uninitiated. It requires different "reading" skills.

To make sense of the anarchy and chaos, readers need to become creators. This means following links around so that they can discover different themes, concepts, and outcomes. "Interactive Storytime" is an early example. It tells stories with narration, print, music, sound effects, and graphics. Children can click on any object and connect spelling to the pronunciation.

Literature has traditionally had a linear progression worked out in advance by the author. The reader brought background knowledge and a unique interpretation to what the author had written. But it was the author who provided the basic sequential structure that pushed all readers in the same direction. Computer-based multidimensional literature is quite different. The reader shapes the story line by choosing the next expository sequence from a number of possibilities.

With early versions of interactive computer-based literature, readers are connected to a vast web of printed text, sound, graphics, and lifelike video. When key words or images are highlighted on a computer screen, the reader uses a mouse (or finger on a touch screen) to click on what he or she wants next, and the reader hops into a new place in the story, causing different outcomes. With a virtual-reality format, the "reader" uses his or her whole body to interact with the story. Whatever the configuration, interactive literature causes the user to break down some of the walls that usually separate the reader from what's being read.

The forking paths in this electronic literature pose new problems for readers—like how do you know when you have finished reading when you can just keep going all over the place? Judy Malloy's *Its Name Was Penelope*, for example, shuffles four hundred pages of a fictional woman's memories so that they come together very differently every time you read it. The ambiguity of these programs isn't as bothersome as it used to be.

Today, children are used to television and computer programs that deal with quick movement between short segments of information. In addition, many video games and computer simulations require students to wander in a maze of ideas. As a result, children are usually not as disoriented by the various forms of interactive literature as adults.

Odd varieties of e-stories can be found on the Internet. Some are free, some are comparable to a traditional book in price, and others require a multimedia or virtual-reality platform. Many of these efforts at constructing interactive stories are more like interactive comic books than literature. Programs are becoming more sophisticated and are giving us some advance warning of a new literary genre. One thing is for sure: this is something important for the future of curriculum and instruction.

ONLINE PEER TUTORING

Both off- or online peer tutoring involve several methods. In *cross-age tutoring*, older students tutor younger students. In *cross-ability tutoring*, a student who has a good grasp of the subject can tutor a student who is struggling. *Reciprocal tutoring* involves a structure for interaction that is tied to specific academic goals (Grant, 2009).

CONVEYING MEANING WITH POWERFUL VISUAL MODELS

One way to enhance the power and permanency of what we learn is to use visually based mental models in conjunction with the printed word. Inferences drawn from visually intensive media can lead to more profound thinking. In fact, children often rely on their perceptual (visual) learning even if their conceptual knowledge contradicts it. In other words, even when what's being presented runs contrary to verbal explanations, potent visual experiences can push viewers to accept what is presented. Children can become adept at extracting meaning from the conventions of video, film, or animation—zooms, pans, tilts, fade-outs, and flashbacks. But distinguishing fact from fiction is more difficult.

The ability to understand what's being presented visually is becoming ever more central to learning and to our society. Most of the time, children construct meaning for television, film, computer, or Internet content without even thinking about it. They may not be critical consumers, but they attend to stimuli and extract meaning from subtle messages. The underlying message children often get from the mass media is that viewers should consume as much as possible while changing as little as possible. How well content is understood varies according to similarities between the viewers and the content. Viewers' needs, interests, and ages are other important factors. Sorting through the themes of mental conservatism and material addition requires carefully developed thinking skills.

Meaning in any medium is constructed by each participant at several levels. For better or for worse, broadcast television used to provide us with a common culture. When viewers share a common visual culture, they must also share a similar set of tools and processes for interpreting these signals (construction of meaning, information processing, interpretation, and evaluation). The greater the experiential background in the culture being represented, the greater the understanding. The ability to make subtle judgments about what is going on in any medium is a developmental outcome that proceeds from stage to stage with an accumulation of experience.

Relying on a host of cognitive inputs, individuals select and interpret the raw data of experience to produce a personal understanding of reality. What is understood while viewing depends on the interplay of images and social conditions. Physical stimuli, human psychology, and information processing schemes taught by this culture help each person make sense of the world. In this respect, reacting to the content of an electronic medium is no different from any other experience in life. It is just as possible to internalize ideas from electronic visual imagery as it is from conversation, print, or personal experience. It's just that comprehension occurs differently.

Reflective thought and imaginative active play are an important part of the growth process of a child. Even with a "lean-back," passive medium like television, children must do active work as they watch, make sense of its contents, and utilize its messages. With a "lean-forward" medium like the Internet, this work is fairly evident. Evaluative activities include judging and assigning worth, assessing what is admired, and deciding what positive and negative impressions should be assigned to the content. In this sense, children are active participants in determining meaning in any medium.

ADULTS INFLUENCE HOW CHILDREN LEARN TO ASSESS MEDIA MESSAGES

Although children learn best if they take an active role in their own learning, parents, teachers, and other adults are major influences. They can significantly affect what information children gather from television, film, or the Internet. Whatever their age, critical users of media should be able to:

- Understand the grammar and syntax of a medium as expressed in different program forms
- Analyze the pervasive appeals of advertising
- Compare similar presentations or those with similar purposes in different media
- Identify values in language, characterization, conflict resolution, and sound/visual images
- Utilize strategies for the management of duration of viewing and program choices
- Identify elements in dramatic presentations associated with the concepts of plot, story line, theme, characterizations, motivation, program formats, and production values

Parents and teachers can affect children's interest in media messages and help them learn how to process information. Good modeling behavior, explaining content, and showing how the content relates to student interests are just a few examples of how adults can provide positive viewing motivation. Adults can also exhibit an informed response by pointing out misleading messages—without building curiosity for undesirable programs.

The viewing, computer, and Internet using habits of families play a large role in determining how children approach a medium. The length of time parents spend watching television, the kinds of programs viewed, and the reactions of parents and siblings to programming messages all have a large influence on the child. If adults read and there are books, magazines, and newspapers around the house, children will pay more attention to print. Influencing what children view on television or the Internet may be done by setting rules about what may or may not be watched, interacting with children during viewing, and modeling certain content choices. A tip for parents: it's usually a good idea to keep the computer in the family room.

Whether or not co-viewing is taking place, the viewing choices of adults in a child's life (parents, teachers, etc.) set an example for children. If, for example, parents are heavy watchers of public television or news programming, then children are more likely to respond favorably to this content. If parents make informed, intelligent use of the Internet, then children are likely to build on that model. Influencing the settings in which children watch TV or use the computer is also a factor. Turning the TV set off during meals, for example, sets a family priority.

Families can also seek a more open and equal approach to choosing television shows—interacting before, during, and after the program. When it comes to the Internet, keep the computer in the family room rather than in a private, isolated space. Time limits must be placed on today's electronic gadgets. Parents can organize formal or informal group activities outside the house that provide alternatives to Internet use or TV viewing.

It is increasingly clear that the education of children is a shared responsibility. Parents obviously play a central role and they need connections with what's going on in the schools. Working together, parents and teachers can use television, computers, and the Internet to encourage students to become more intelligent media consumers. When it comes to schooling, it is teachers who will be the ones called on to make the educational connections entwining varieties of print and visual media with the basic curriculum.

COMMUNICATIONS TECHNOLOGY AND PUBLIC CONVERSATIONS

A democratic community is defined by the quality of its educational institutions and its public conversations. Democracy often becomes what it pays attention to. American national values, supported by our Constitution, require an educated citizenry that can think and respond to leaders and are willing to actively go beyond the obvious. Patriotism isn't just the flag and stern rhetoric; it's a thinking, decent, and literate society. Exercising citizenship in a world of accelerated change requires the preservation of our human values.

Ignoring the societal implications of technology means ignoring looming changes. Whether it's technologically induced passivity or the seductive charms of believing in simplistic technological solutions, it is only through the educational process that people can gain a heightened awareness of bright human and technological possibilities. The question that we need to answer is, how might the technology be used to spark a renaissance in human learning and communication?

The long-term implications of recent changes in information and communications technology are important, if not frightening. The convergence of technologies is causing a major change in societal behaviors, lifestyles, and thinking patterns. With few people monitoring digital technology or theorizing its health, the human race is being forced to swim in an electronic sea of information and ideas. In today's world, there is little question that reality is being shaped by electronic information and electronic illusions.

ACTIVITIES FOR MAKING SENSE OUT OF VISUAL MEDIA

1. *Help students critically view what they see.*

   Decoding visual stimuli and learning from visual images require practice. Seeing an image does not automatically ensure learning from it. Students must be guided in decoding and looking critically at what they view. One technique is to have students "read" the image on various levels. Students identify individual elements and classify them into various categories, then relate the whole to their own experiences, drawing inferences and creating new conceptualizations from what they have learned.

   Encourage students to look at the plot and story line. Identify the message of the program. What symbols (camera techniques, motion sequences, setting, lighting, etc.) does the program use to make its message? What the director does to highlight packaging, color, and images influences consumers and often distorts reality. Analyze and discuss commercials in different media. How many minutes of ads appear in an hour? How many ads do you have to sort through before you can watch a program or use a search engine to get to some Web sites? What should be done about the ad glut?

2. *Create a scrapbook of media clippings.*

   Have students keep a scrapbook of newspaper and magazine clippings on computers, the Internet, Facebook, Google, television, and some of the other inhabitants of cyberspace. Newspapers and magazines are a good source of articles. The *New York Times* Science section is a good example for upper-grade students. Ask students to paraphrase, draw a picture, or map out a personal interpretation of an interesting technology article. Share these with other students.

3. *Create new images from the old.*

Have students take rather mundane photographs and multiply the image, or combine it with others, in a way that makes the photos interesting. Through the act of observing, it is possible to build a common body of experiences, humor, feeling, and originality. And through collaborative efforts, students can expand on ideas and make the group process come alive.

4. *Role-play communicating with extraterrestrial life.*

Directions for students: If extraterrestrial life has already contacted us, think about how to respond. Think creatively and scientifically about how you would explain this planet to some inquisitive aliens. Explain human life and media devices; try to view our planet as a whole.

5. *Use debate for critical thought.*

Debating is a communications model that can serve as a lively facilitator for concept building. Take a current and relevant topic, and formally debate it online or face-to-face. This can serve as an important speech and language extension. For example, the class can discuss how mass media can support everything from commercialism to public conformity and the technological control of society. The discussion can serve as a blend of technology, social studies, science, and the humanities.

Electronic media and social patterns are constantly shifting through various stages of acceptance and use. Communications now come in many forms and from many locations—served up on a variety of digital devices. So it is little wonder that an important instructional goal is giving young people the skills needed to swim through today's technological crosscurrents.

DIFFERENT MEDIA SYMBOL SYSTEMS

Print and visually intensive media take different approaches to communicating meaning. Print relies on the reader's ability to interpret abstract symbols. A video or computer screen is more direct. Whatever the medium, thinking and learning are based on internal symbolic representations and the mental interpretation of those symbols. When they are used in combination, one medium can amplify another.

We live in a complex society dependent on rapid communication and information access. Lifelike visual symbol systems are comprised in part of story structure, pace, sound track, color, and conceptual difficulty. Computers, the Internet, television, and digital devices are rapidly becoming our dominant cultural tools for selecting, gathering, storing, and conveying knowledge in representational forms (Levy, 2011).

Various electronic symbol systems play a central role in modern communications. It is important that students begin to develop the skills necessary for interpreting and processing the full range of media messages. Symbolically different presentations of media vary as to the mental skills of processing they require. Each individual learns to use a media's symbolic forms for purposes of internal representation.

To even begin to read, for example, a child needs to know something about thought-symbol relationships. To move beneath the surface of electronic imagery requires some of the same understandings. It takes skill to break free from a wash of images and electronically induced visual quicksand. These skills don't just develop naturally; training is required to develop critical media consumers who are literate in interpreting and processing print or visual images.

Unlike direct experience, print or visual representation is always coded within a symbol system. Learning to understand that the system cultivates the mental skills necessary for gathering and assimilating internal representations is important. Each communications and information medium makes use of its own distinctive technology for gathering, encoding, sorting, and conveying its contents associated with different situations. The technological mode of a medium affects the interaction with its users—just as the method for transmitting content affects the knowledge acquired.

The closer the match between the way information is presented and the way it can be mentally represented, the easier it is to learn. Better communication means easier processing and more transfer. At its best, a medium gets out of your way and lets you get directly at the issues. New educational choices are being laid open by electronic technologies. Understanding and employing these technological forces require interpreting new media possibilities from a unique and critical perspective.

UNDERSTANDING AND CREATING ELECTRONIC MESSAGES

Understanding media conventions helps cultivate mental tools of thought. In any medium, this gives the viewer new ways of handling and exploring the world. The ability to interpret the action and messages requires going beyond the surface to understanding the deep structure of the medium. Understanding the practical and philosophical nuances of a medium moves its consumers in the direction of mastery.

Simply seeing an image does not have much to do with learning from it. The levels of knowledge and skill that children bring with them to the viewing situation determine the areas of knowledge and skill development acquired. Just as with reading print, decoding visually intensive stimuli and learning from visual images require practice.

Students can be guided in decoding and looking critically at what they view. One technique is to have students "read" the image on various levels. Students identify individual elements, classify them into various categories, and then relate the whole to their own experiences. They can then draw inferences and create new conceptualizations from what they have learned.

Planning, visualizing, and developing a production allow students to critically sort out and use media techniques to relay meaning. Young producers should be encouraged to open their eyes to the world and visually experience what's out there. By realizing their ideas through media production, students learn to redefine space and time as they use media attributes such as structure, sound, color, pacing, and imaging.

The field of technology and its educational associates are in a period of introspection, self-doubt, and great expectations. In a world awash with different types of educational media, theoretical guidelines are needed as much as specific instructional methods. It is dangerous to function in a theory- or research-deprived vacuum because there can spring up rituals that are worse than those drained away. As schools are faced with aggressive marketing for electronic devices, we must ensure that a pedagogical plan that incorporates technology is in place.

For technological tools to reach their promise, there are required close connections among educational research, theory, and classroom practice. Across the curriculum, new standards that place a high premium on creative and critical thinking are needed. So it is clear that the curriculum and professional development will pay even closer attention to such skills.

Reaching students requires opening students' eyes to things they might not have thought of on their own. This means using technological tools as capable collaborators for tapping into real experience, fantasies, and personal visions. This way, previously obscure concepts can become comprehensible, with greater depth, at an earlier age.

Technology and metacognitive strategies can come together as students search for data, solve problems, and graphically simulate their way through multiple levels of abstraction. The combination of thoughtful strategies and the enabling features of media tools can achieve more lasting cognitive change and improved performance.

SOCIAL EQUITY AND A MODERN PHILOSOPHY OF TEACHING

When it comes to solving our educational problems, technology isn't the only thing. But it is an important thing. As we put together the technological components that provide access to a truly individualized set of learning experiences, it is important to develop a modern philosophy of teaching, learning, and social equity. While new information and communications technologies have the potential to make society more equal, they sometimes have the opposite effect. As we enter new technological worlds, everyone must have access.

Many American school districts lack the money to train teachers to use digital technology effectively. So in some schools, children are still taught to use the computer primarily for typing, drill, and workbook-like practice. In contrast, affluent schools often encourage students to use digital technology for creative exploration—like designing multimedia presentations and collaborating with classmates in problem-solving experimentation. Everyone deserves access to a provocative and challenging curriculum. To become an equal instrument of educational reform, technology must do more than just reinforce a two-tier system of education. Otherwise, many children will face a discouraging picture of technological inequality.

There are serious social consequences surrounding the inequalities of access to telecommunications and advanced information technology. Future connections to faculty, other students, databases, and library resources will change the way that information is created, accessed, and transmitted. Those denied access may have their academic ambitions stifled, causing them to fall farther and farther behind. The challenge is to make sure that this information is available for all in a twenty-first-century version of the public library.

Digital technology gives us the ability to change the tone and priorities of gathering information and learning in a democratic society. Taking the right path requires learning to use what's available today and building a social and educational infrastructure that can travel the knowledge highways of the future.

Working with students online, we have found computer simulations that simulate invisible things like molecular reactions and static electricity. In addition, with role-playing interactive activities from around the world, it is possible to foster thinking skills and collaboration.

Electronically connecting the human mind to people and global information resources may shift human consciousness in ways similar to what occurred in moving from an oral to a written culture. The ultimate consequences are unclear. But the development of basic skills, habits of the mind, wisdom, and traits of character will be increasingly affected by the technology (Roblyer and Doering, 2010).

The curriculum materials that are most effective and most popular are those that provide for social interaction and problem solving. Information can be embedded in visual narratives to create contexts that give meaning to dry facts.

Interactive digital technology can challenge students on many levels and even serve as a training ground for responsibility, persistence, and collaborative inquiry. It's relatively easy to buy the hardware and get children interested. The difficult thing is to connect to deep learning in a manner that advances curriculum goals.

New technology is a double-edged sword. Laptops can be used to record or take notes on the day's activities and presentations. They can also be a distraction as students check e-mail or Facebook; a few even use the technology to cheat during class. Cell phones can also be used to gather useful educational information and record important parts of a class. But they can also be brazenly used to send instant messages and waste time texting during class.

To stay on a useful curriculum and instructional path at school, it is important to recognize the fact that many students today have been brought up in an age of whiz-bang gadgets. Their approach to media and daily life is one of constant contact and multitasking. Technological expertise and curiosity are one thing; constant distraction quite another.

On the first day of class, teachers need to set and post specific rules and specific consequences for off-task activities. Decide if or when cell phones or laptops can be used during class. Remember to tell students if you don't want a lesson to be recorded. Do not leave it open for debate — enforce the posted rules consistently and fairly.

Schools need more adults than ever: teachers, aides, parents, older students, and more. Technological tools can get in the way of learning. But on the positive side, they can be a unique and useful supplement that allows teachers to enhance their lessons and try out some new things.

LEARNING TO EVALUATE ONLINE ACTIVITIES AND SOFTWARE

Curriculum is a cooperative and interactive venture between students and teachers. On both the individual and social levels, those directly involved with the process must be taken seriously. Working together, they can decide what benefits are gained from particular software programs. After all, the software user is in the best position to decide if the program is taking people out of the process — or whether learners are in control of the computers. Good software programs let students learn together at their own pace — visualizing, talking together, and explaining abstract concepts so that they can relate them to real-life situations.

There are time-consuming evaluation issues surrounding the multitude of software programs to be dealt with. Multimedia, simulation, microworlds, word processing, interactive literature, spreadsheets, database managers, expert (AI) systems, or getting the computer in contact with the outside world all increase the potential for influencing impressionable minds. That is too large a universe for the teacher to figure out alone. Teachers can help one another. Another thing that helps the task become more approachable is getting the students to take on some of the responsibility.

Children can learn to critique everything from computer software to Web sites much as they learned to critique the dominant media of yesteryear—books. One of the first tenets of book review criticism is to critique what is usually taken for granted. Also, having at least a little affection for what is being reviewed helps. Students can do book reports, review computer software, and discuss the quality of sites on the Internet. It helps if they sift through some of the software reviews in newspapers, magazines, and journals both online and off-line.

Examining online activities and software: Students can quickly check to see if the flow of a program makes sense. Next, they can try out the software as they think a successful or unsuccessful student might. What happens when mistakes are made? How are the graphics? Do you think you can learn anything from this? Is it exciting?

Without question, teachers and students are the ones who experience the consequences of making good or bad choices in software selection. And they are the ones who most quickly learn the consequences of poor choices.

CRITERIA FOR EVALUATING E-ACTIVITIES

Teachers can apply the same assessment techniques used on other instructional materials when they evaluate courseware. The following list is an example.

1. Does the activity meet the age and attention demands of your students?
2. Does it hold the student's interest?
3. Do the programs, activities, or simulation games develop, supplement, or enhance curricular skills?
4. Does the work require adult supervision or instruction?
5. Children need to actively control what the program does. To what extent does the program allow this?
6. Can the courseware be modified to meet individual learning requirements?
7. Can it be adjusted to the learning styles of the user?
8. Does the program have animated graphics that enliven the lesson?
9. Does it meet instructional objectives and is it educationally sound?
10. Does the activity or program involve higher-level thinking and problem solving?

Student Evaluation Checklist

Name of student evaluator(s)

_____

Name of software program

_____

Publisher _____ Subject _____

1. How long did the activity take? _____ minutes
2. Did you need to ask for help doing the work?

   _____

3. What skills do you think the activity tried to teach?

   _____

   Please circle the word that best answers the question.

4. Was it fun to use? yes no somewhat not very
5. Were the directions clear? yes no somewhat not very
6. Was it easy to use? yes no somewhat not very
7. Were the graphics (pictures) good? yes no somewhat not very
8. Did the activity get you really involved? yes no somewhat not very
9. Were you able to make choices in the ? yes no
10. What mistakes did you make?

    _____

11. What happed when you made a mistake?

    _____

12. What was the most interesting part of the activity?

    _____

13. What did you like least?

    _____

14. What's a good tip to give a friend who's getting started with this activity?

    _____

Extended work:

- Make up a quiz about the particular computer program or online activity and give the questions to other students in the class who have used it.
- Create your own sound track for part of the activity.
- Make up a student guide for the activity. Use your own directions and illustrations.
- Write or dramatize an interview with one of the characters in a television program or in a movie.
- Interview other students who have used the activity and write their responses.
- Write a review of the activity and post it online.

Remember, there are many "top ten" or "best of" lists out there for consideration.

SERVING PEDAGOGY

The curriculum should drive the technology rather than the other way around. The most effective use of such tools occurs when desired learning outcomes are figured out first. Once standards have been set, you can decide what technological applications will help you reach your goals. Technology can help when it serves clear educational goals. But there is much work to be done—put an *e* and a dash in front of "education." However, by working together, teachers can learn from one another, push on to other innovations, and build a medium worthy of our students (Willard, 2002).

Converging communication technologies can serve as a great public resource. Commercial profit alone should not determine how these new technologies will be exploited. The airwaves and the information highways are owned by the public. Emerging public utilities must show a concern for learning and responsible social action. Any new media system is a public trust that should enable students to become intelligent and informed citizens.

In today's world, children grow up interacting with electronic media as much as they interact with print or with people. Unfortunately, much of the programming is not only violent, repetitious, and mindless, but it also distracts students from more important literacy and physical exercise activities. New technologies, software, and interactive media amplify everything. Dealing with these new digital realities requires a new approach to curriculum and instruction. It also requires a heightened sense of social responsibility on the part of those in control of programming.

Not only has the media changed but also how we now live in a society that is ruled by profits. It is the time to go back to considering the public interest and devising rules to ensure that the mass media takes responsibility for the fact that it influences the foundation on which formal learning takes place.

TIPS FOR USING TECHNOLOGY

- Technology is an important thing, but not the only thing.
- Put the learning piece in place first.
- Don't panic or be intimidated by technology.
- Make mistakes and learn from your failures.
- Don't be afraid to learn from your students.
- Bring everybody along; leave no one behind.
- Teach your teachers; invest in teacher training.
- Two-way is the only way. Foster active conversation.
- Have fun. Be sure that there is some joy in it.

Remember, both real and imaginary factors can stir people to action.

The human imagination can be enhanced by technology-based instruction in a way that makes actual experiences more meaningful. With computer control, you can speed it up, slow it down, go into an atom, or go back into the past. On occasion, the experience can even transcend print or actual experience as an analytical tool.

LOOKING IN THE DIRECTION OF TOMORROW

Amid all the commercial maneuvering, new media technologies have the potential for empowering students to take more control of their learning. It can also extend our reach for new knowledge and assist in the search for new ways of learning.

Digital technology not only can make information more visually intriguing, but it also can provide two-way communication with live or artificially intelligent experts. Tutoring, for example, will be done by live, recorded, or computer-composed experts.

Digital interactive storytelling techniques will allow plotlines to evolve in almost infinite directions. Characters can even be programmed to surprise us in ways that have never been written. Lessons can play out cognitive strengths. There are at least three ways to think of spelling a word, for example. One is to picture it. This may be thought of as an experiential kinesthetic approach. Another way is "to sound a word out," an audio approach. A third approach is visual. You see the word in your mind and spell it.

It is important to recognize the fact that digital textuality is quite different from what's found in print culture. It has a different logic and takes a different approach to the construction of knowledge. Although digital literacy is still in its infancy, it has already shown real promise and serious limitations. The result is movement toward a new, hybrid cultural landscape (Doueihi, 2011).

Computer-generated technology has already proved that it can give the user a sense of being in another reality. From airline pilots to surgeons, computer simulations have been used to hone skills for years. As the technology improves and the prices come down, real possibilities for learning open up.

Within the multisensory world of virtual reality, people can see, hear, and touch objects. Some of the applications being developed involve what has been called "telepresence," which gives the operator the sensation of putting his or her hands and eyes in a remote location. One could, for example, send a robot to Mars or the bottom of the ocean, control the action, see what the robot sees, and feel what it feels.

Can we predict where all this whiz-bang technology will take us? The best advice is to pursue multiple paths and not be afraid to change direction. In this way, we can push back the horizon of predictability. The more unsettled things become, the more important it is to have a range of possibilities. Even luck is the residue of design. If the implications of multiple versions of the future are thought through, it is bound to be good preparation for whatever happens.

OPPORTUNITIES TODAY AND THE CHALLENGES AHEAD

When considered collectively, digital technology is the most powerful representational medium ever invented. It should be put to the highest tasks of society. As far as the schools are concerned, this means using technology to motivate students to explore school subjects with passionate curiosity.

Whether it's in or out of the classroom, many school-age youngsters in developed countries spend much of their time engaged with media. It often becomes their main source of information, knowledge, and experience. They may say that what really counts is real-life encounters, but the reality is that many are more strongly influenced by online activity.

Digital devices will continue to evolve in ways that extend human capabilities and compensate for the limits of the human mind. Clearly, dealing with emerging digital technologies is one of the many challenges that teachers will face in the twenty-first century. We often lament the fact that new teachers have not been provided the training to use new technologies available to them.

Some teachers are still coming through teacher education programs that did not prepare them adequately to integrate digital technology with instructional tasks. In addition, some states pay little attention to the in-service needs of their teachers. This is not a question of remediation. Rather, it is the fact that any profession requires its members to keep up to date with new findings and cutting-edge technology. College classes and outside experts can help. But schools need to acquire their own in-house capacity for helping teachers with professional development.

Increasingly, today's teachers and students have to navigate a world that is networked and global. Being able to work with others online and off-line matters. Collaborators can be sitting next to you—or they can be halfway around the world. In the future, understanding and creating with digital tools will be as important as basic reading, writing, and math skills (Ferriter and Garry, 2010).

The future of education and technology is bound to be invaded by the present. From social networks to search engines, digital tools will continue to redefine literacy and reshape the architecture of learning. A wide range of new technological tools are already helping students learn in different ways—while permitting them to explore a much broader world of knowledge and learning. There is much more to come.

Perhaps artificial intelligence can be used to help enhance and develop the human variety. But since we still don't have a clear understanding of human *or* machine consciousness, it will take a while to really make a big difference. Then again, it may not take too long. After all, we have already become tone deaf to the difference between a human and an AI-assisted computer voice (Christian, 2011).

Today, mobile gadgets and social media are redefining how the Web and its technological associates are used. As far as tomorrow is concerned, we can only begin to imagine how new technologies and approaches will change the future of learning and life. To successfully sail through the crosscurrents of such a transitional age requires the development of stronger intellectual habits and a willingness to learn about what's going on in a technologically intensive world.

SUMMARY, CONCLUSION, AND LOOKING AHEAD

Learning to separate noise from knowledge is increasingly important in this age of too much information. Making better use of "knowledge machines" (digital technology) means going well beyond electronic workbooks or surfing the Internet to collaboratively explore problems and tinker with disparate ideas. The good news is that it's at least *possible* for technological tools to provide a vehicle for building on students' natural curiosity and promoting real learning through active engagement and collaborative inquiry.

The human mind can create beyond either what it intends or what it can foresee. Combinations of electronic media will be with us no matter how far the electronic environment expands. The problem is being sure that it works to human advantage. The informing power of technological tools can help change the schools. It can also make learning come alive and breathe wisdom into instructional activities (Nelson and Erlandson, 2012).

Technological application goes a long way toward explaining the shape of everyone's world today. Along the path to the future, many people have grown used to having technology between them and reality. We shape digital technologies and at the same time, they shape us. Along the way, many strands of possibilities shape the future of people's lives. Clearly, the focus of education must be shifted in a way that helps prepare students for a future that is vastly different from what their teachers have known.

We know that technologies like the Internet are fragmenting the thought processes of young people. Also, there is less and less time for reflection and quiet thought. But no matter where all the changes take us, reasoning, communication, and teamwork skills are bound to go hand in hand with taking an active part in shaping the future.

Harmonizing students' present with the future requires more than reinventing the schools. In America, for example, not only are some schools failing, but the home environment and society are also failing.

Many children are behind on their first day of school, so efforts to improve schooling must extend before and beyond the classroom door. For all learners to thrive academically, it helps to have the benefits of preschool, high-quality teachers, health care, and engaged family support.

Without broad assistance, the schools will not be able to provide a good education for all students. New technologies are filled with possibility. But just because we come up with more and more ingenious ways of communicating doesn't mean that we understand much about what's being communicated.

Is access to an infinite amount of information infinitely valuable or does it simply lead to the collapse of clear and well-thought-out meaning? Whatever the combination of answers, uncontrolled technological change is a problem—and for new media to contribute, it has to have a human face. Although the technology-intensive educational path to the future may be bumpy, it doesn't have to be gloomy. Clearly, dedicated teachers who understand and know how to use their high-tech tools can make a real difference.

Although we live in an information age, a clear understanding of the nature of information remains elusive. With or without an understanding of the concept, increasing the information flow presents at least as many problems as it provides opportunities (Gleick, 2011). The same thing might be said about technology in general. What's needed is a controlling vision that can help explain concepts related to information, technological innovation, and implications for education.

With or without a grand plan for the future, educators can strive to educate the whole person to be productive in a rapidly changing, technology-intensive, democratic society.

> We have trod the face of the Moon, touched the nethermost pit of the sea, and can link minds across vast distances. . . . But for all that, it's not so much our technology, but what we believe, that will determine our fate. —Tim Flannery

SUGGESTED RESOURCES

Brockman, J. (Ed.). (2011). *Is the Internet changing the way you think? The Net's impact on our minds and future*. New York: HarperCollins.

Brown, J., and P. Duduid. (2000). *The social life of information*. Boston: Harvard Business School Press.

Grosswiler, P. (Ed.). (2010). *Transforming McLuhan: Cultural, critical, and postmodern perspectives*. New York: Peter Lang.

Lehrer, J. (2009). *How we decide*. New York: Houghton Mifflin Harcourt.

National Educational Technology Standards for Students. (2000). *Connecting curriculum and technology*. Eugene, OR: International Society for Technology in Education.

Turkle, S. (2011). *Why we expect more from technology and less from each other*. New York: Basic Books.

REFERENCES

Bellance, J., and R. Brandt (Eds). (2010). *21st century skills: Rethinking how students learn*. Bloomington, IN: Solution Tree Press.

Caine, R., and G. Caine. (2011). *Natural learning for a connected world: Education, technology, and the human brain*. New York: Teachers College Press.

Christian, B. (2011). *The most human human: What talking with computers teaches us about what it means to be alive*. New York: Doubleday.

Doueihi, M. (2011). *Digital cultures*. Cambridge, MA: Harvard University Press.

Ferriter, W., and A. Garry. (2010). *Teaching the igeneration: 5 easy ways to introduce essential skills with web 2.0 tools*. Bloomington, IN: Solution Tree Press.

Flannery, T. (2011). *Here on earth: A natural history of the planet*. New York: Atlantic Monthly Press.

Gleick, J. (2011). *The information: A history, a theory, a flood*. New York: Pantheon Books.

Grant, G. (2009). *Hope and despair in the American city: Why there are no bad schools in Raleigh*. Cambridge, MA: Harvard University Press.

Levy, S. (2011). *In the plex: How Google thinks, works, and shapes our lives*. New York: Simon & Schuster.

Logan, R. K. (2010). *Understanding new media: Extending Marshall McLuhan*. New York: Peter Lang.

Nelson, B. C., and B. E. Erlandson. (2012). *Design for learning in virtual worlds (interdisciplinary approaches to educational technology)*. New York: Routledge.

Roblyer, M., and A. Doering. (2010). *Integrating educational technology into teaching*. Boston: Allyn & Bacon.

Rose, E. (2010). Continuous partial attention: Reconsidering the role of online learning in the age of interruption. *Educational Technology* 50, no. 4 (July/August).

West, D. (2012). *Digital schools: How technology can transform education*. Washington, DC: Brookings Institution Press.

Willard, N. (2002). *Computer ethics, etiquette, and safety for the 21st-century student*. Eugene, OR: International Society for Technology in Education.

FIVE

Science and Math

Focus, Inquiry, and Creative Problem Solving

Math and science are the engines of innovation. With these engines we can lead the world. We must demystify math and science so that all students feel the joy that follows understanding. —Nobel Prize Laureate Michael Brown

It is always helpful to have some familiarity with the thinking processes that are part of science and mathematics. When it comes to understanding an increasingly complex and changing world, everyone can profit from scientific and mathematical reasoning. The scientific method, for example, is a thinking process that can help anyone approach the wide range of possibilities that occurs daily (Froschauer and Bigelow, 2012).

There are as many ways to think about "twenty-first-century skills" as there are ways to think about science and mathematics instruction. Here, we limit ourselves to basic content areas, emerging topics, thinking skills, and life skills such as adaptability, teamwork, and social responsibility. Close attention is also paid to K–8 classrooms and the negative consequences that stem from isolating science and math from humanism.

At all levels, the offshoots of science and math—like information and communications technology—are moving closer to the center of the instructional stage. As far as the subjects of science and math are concerned, it is important that students understand at least some of the ideas and applications of experts in the field. It also helps if learners are encouraged to do creative things with their own informed opinions, insights, and conclusions.

Pushing the sphere of what's known is the essence of creativity and innovation. Tomorrow's schools and workplaces are bound to highly value those who continually search for fresh ideas and attempt to do new

87

things. Creating fresh ideas and products requires individuals and groups who can go beyond conventional wisdom, take risks, and learn from mistakes (Dweck, 2006).

Innovative change is not always immediate and total. It is possible, for example, to work on the incremental improvements right now, while simultaneously thinking far ahead. Innovation takes many forms. It ranges from Facebook's "move fast and break things," to Bell Labs' "move deliberately and build things." Fast or slow, short or long term, scientific reasoning and mathematical problem solving are keys to technological and engineering success.

Even in the primary grades, it is important for students to realize that scientific and mathematical ideas have a thought-provoking role to play in everything from current affairs to music, sports, and literature (Bybee, 2010).

When it comes to using the imagination to solve problems in new ways, mastering traditional science and math content at school goes only so far. Interacting imaginatively with others and communicating individual values are all part of the process.

TOO IMPORTANT TO BE LEFT TO EXPERTS

Whether they are done individually or in groups, formally or informally, science/math activities and their technological associates are simply too important to be left to the experts.

Many teachers of science and mathematics at the elementary school level have to teach dozens of topics and subjects. So, it should not come as a surprise to find out that many have not received specialist training in every subject. (By the middle grades, specialists are more common.) Still, when it comes to teaching science and math, it is important for all teachers to have the intellectual tools needed to help children learn and apply age-appropriate concepts.

Students at any age can learn to ask big questions and think about grand concepts. In fact, those who work deeply with science and math at an early age are more likely to be creative in these subjects later on (Neagoy, 2012). Technologies like the Internet have made it possible for anyone to learn throughout their lives.

Curiosity and thoughtful engagement drive intellectual development in science and math. Only a small percentage of children may become scientists or mathematicians, but everyone must know enough to apply the intellectual tools that are part of these subjects.

Major goals of science and math education in the twenty-first century include helping students develop more self-understanding and move in the direction of responsible citizenship. Along the way, it is important to recognize that new technologies are altering the way knowledge is conveyed.

CORE CURRICULUM STANDARDS FOR SCIENCE AND MATHEMATICS

The National Research Council (NRC) has published *A Framework for K–12 Science Education: Practices, Crosscutting Concepts, and Core Ideas* (2011). This publication takes one of the most important steps forward in science and math education since the National Science Standards (1995) and the National Mathematics Standards (2001). The NRC constructed the science framework and is working on the next generation of science standards.

The standards bring an imaginative perspective to learning science and math, and emphasize the importance of challenging students in *doing* science and mathematics, not just learning content.

The science framework identifies key scientific ideas and practices that all students should learn. Among other things, it is designed to help students gradually develop their knowledge of core ideas in four interdisciplinary areas over multiple years, rather than gaining shallow knowledge by covering many topics.

The latest science framework strongly emphasizes the ways students carry out science investigations and encourages arguments based on evidence (National Academy Press, 2011).

The goal of the new standards is to ensure that all students have an appreciation for the beauty and wonder of science and mathematics. Students should have the capacity to discuss and think critically about science- and math-related issues and eventually pursue careers in science, math, and engineering. Currently, science and math in the United States lack a common vision of what students should know and be able to do.

Over the last few decades, both teaching methods and subject matter content have changed. So have the textbooks. Increasingly, students have e-textbooks, e-books, and e-zines that can be accessed on all kinds of mobile devices. Still, hard-copy books have a role to play in any pedagogical version of the future. It is up to educators to decide on the technological mix that works best in different situations.

Although legislators may be dazzled by lobbyists for high-tech companies, there is little proof that technology alone improves learning. Also, there are times when in order to benefit from new technologies, we need to use them less. Some Silicon Valley firms, for instance, make sure that e-mail is not available one day a week to allow their employees to collaborate in person on team projects and concentrate on more important tasks.

SCIENCE, MATH, AND THE SCHOOL CURRICULUM

The evolving nature of science and mathematics is one of the reasons for so much debate within the scientific community and in the general public. As far as classroom-based discussion, experiments, and computations are concerned, students must learn how to collaboratively put the skills they learn into practice. All these points connect to the subject matter standards.

Take science education as an example: the science interdisciplinary areas include life science, physical science, earth/space science, engineering, technology, and the application of science. Some core ideas that cut across these fields include matter, interactions, and energy. Students understand that the same idea is relevant in many fields. These concepts should become familiar as students progress from kindergarten through grade 12.

Both the science and the math standards emphasize key practices that students should learn: asking questions, defining problems, and analyzing and interpreting data. Other important practices include explaining ideas and designing solutions. These practices need to be linked with the study of interdisciplinary core ideas and applied throughout students' education.

GUIDING PRINCIPLES FOR MATHEMATICS

1. Math ideas should be explored in ways that stimulate curiosity, create enjoyment of math, and develop a depth of understanding. Students should be actively engaged in doing meaningful mathematics, discussing ideas, and applying math in interesting, thought-provoking situations.

2. Math tasks should be designed to challenge students, for instance, by initiating some short- and long-term investigations that connect procedures and skills with conceptual understandings. Tasks should generate active classroom talk, promote conjectures, and lead to an understanding of the necessity of math reasoning.

STANDARDS FOR MATH PRACTICE

1. Make sense of problems and be persistent in trying to solve them.
2. Reason and draw conclusions.
3. Create reasonable arguments.
4. Model with math and science situations.
5. Use appropriate tools.
6. Be precise.
7. Clearly express your reasoning.

8. Interpret results.
9. Report on the conclusions and the reasoning behind them.

MATHEMATICS: A TOOL OF SCIENCE

The initial mystery that attends any journey is: how did the traveler reach the starting point in the first place. —Louise Bogan

Although it is usually best for children to construct knowledge for themselves, we should recognize that students frequently have false understandings about math-related concepts. Some of the misconceptions that students have are natural—some notions are picked up from the media and others, from the home environment. Just have your students draw a picture of a mathematician or a scientist and you will have some graphic evidence of stereotypes. You might also have them keep track of representations in film and on television.

Children have a natural curiosity when it comes to using science and math to examine the natural world. They learn by experiencing things for themselves, building on what they have already learned, and talking with other students about what they are doing. Observing, classifying, measuring, and collecting are just a few examples of the processes that children of all ages can learn and apply (Leinwand, 2012).

UNDERSTANDING SCIENCE AND MATHEMATICS

1. Science and math are methods of thinking and asking questions.

How students make plans, organize their thoughts, analyze data, and solve problems is *doing* science and mathematics. People comfortable with science and math are often comfortable with thinking. The *question* is the cornerstone of all investigation. It guides the learner to a variety of sources revealing previously undetected patterns.

These undiscovered openings can become sources of new questions that can deepen and enhance learning and inquiry. Questions such as, "How can birds fly?" "Why is the sky blue?" or "How many?" have been asked by children throughout history. Obviously, some of their answers were wrong. But the important thing is that the children never stopped asking—they saw and wondered, and sought an answer.

2. Science and math require a knowledge of patterns and relationships.

Children need to recognize the need for the repetition of science and math concepts and to make connections with ideas they know. These relationships help unify the science and math curriculum as each new concept is interwoven with former ideas. Students quickly see how a new concept is similar or different from others already learned. For example, young students soon learn how the basic facts of addition and subtraction are interrelated ($4 + 2 = 6$ and $6 - 2 = 4$). They use their science observation skills to describe, classify, compare, measure, and solve problems.

   3. *Science and math are tools.*

Mathematics is the tool scientists and mathematicians use in their work. It is also used by all of us every day. Students come to understand why they are learning the basic science and math principles and ideas that the school curriculum includes. Like mathematicians and scientists, they also will use science and mathematics tools to solve problems in daily life. They will learn that many careers and occupations are involved with the tools of science and mathematics.

   4. *Science and math are fun (a puzzle).*

Anyone who has ever worked on a puzzle or stimulating problem knows what we're talking about when we say science and mathematics are fun. The stimulating quest for an answer prods one to find a solution.

   5. *Science and math are art forms.*

Defined by harmony and internal order, science and mathematics need to be appreciated as an art form where everything is related and interconnected. Art is often thought to be subjective, and by contrast, objective science and mathematics are often associated with memorized facts and skills. Yet the two are closely related to each other.

Students need to be taught how to appreciate the scientific and mathematical beauty all around them. An example would be exploring fractal instances of science and math in nature. (A fractal is a wispy tangled curve that seems complicated no matter how closely one examines it. The object contains more, but similar, complexity the closer one looks.)

A head of broccoli is one example. If you tear off a tiny piece of the broccoli and look at how it is similar to the larger head, you will soon notice that the two are the same. Each piece of broccoli could be considered an individual fractal or a whole. The piece of broccoli fits the definition of fractal: it appears complicated, yet one can see consistent repetitive artistic patterns.

   6. *Science and math are languages—they are a means of communicating.*

Science and mathematics require being able to use special terms and symbols to represent information like some kind of language. This unique language enhances our ability to communicate across the disciplines of technology, statistics, and other subjects. For example, a young child encountering $3 + 2 = 5$ needs to have the language translated into terms he or she can understand. Language is a window into students' thinking and understanding.

Our job as teachers is to make sure students have carefully defined terms and meaningful symbols. Statisticians may use mathematical symbols that seem foreign to some of us, but after taking a statistics class, we too, can decipher the mathematical language. It's no different for children. Symbolism, along with visual aids such as charts and graphs, is an effective way of expressing science and math ideas to others. Students learn not only to interpret the language of math and science, but, more importantly, to *use* that knowledge.

7. *Science and math are interdisciplinary.*

Students work with the big ideas that connect subjects. Science and mathematics relate to many subjects. Science and technology are the obvious choices. Literature, music, art, social studies, physical education, and just about everything else make use of science and mathematics in some way. If you want to understand what you are reading in the newspaper, for example, you need to be able to read the charts and the graphs taught in science and math classes.

Activities That Help Students Understand Science and Mathematics

1. Science and math are methods of thinking:
   List all the situations outside school in which you used science and math during the past week.
2. Science and math are knowledge of patterns and relationships:
   Show all the ways fifteen objects can be sorted into four piles so that each pile has a different number of objects in it.
3. Science and math are tools:
   Solve these problems using the tools of math and science:

   - Will an orange sink or float in water?
   - What happens when the orange is peeled? Have groups do the experiment and explain their reasoning.

4. Have fun solving a puzzle with science and mathematics:
   With a partner, play a game of cribbage (a card game in which the object is to form combinations for points). Dominoes is another challenging game to play in groups.
5. Use science and math as an art:
   Have a small group of students design a fractal art picture.
6. Apply the language of science and math:
   Divide the class into groups of four or five. Have the groups brainstorm about what they would like to find out about other class members (favorite hobbies, TV programs, kinds of pets, and so forth). Once a topic is agreed on, have them organize and take a survey of all class members. When the data are gathered and compiled, have groups make a clear, descriptive graph that can be posted in the classroom.
7. Design interdisciplinary activities with science and math:
   With a group, design a song using rhythmic format that can be sung, chanted, or rapped. The lyrics can be written and musical notation added.

SCIENCE, MATH, AND TWENTY-FIRST-CENTURY SKILLS

Science and mathematics in the twenty-first century emphasize the processes of good practice, problem solving, reasoning, proof, communications, making connections, and forming scientific and mathematical relationships. Digital technologies are close associates.

Web sites, search engines, data mining, social networks, and other Internet technologies are all part of today's media mix (Andrews, 2012).

A good point for discussion: What can be done about the fact that our digital technologies track, trace, and collect personal consumer data and sell it to profit-making companies? Have central individual privacy rights been violated in cyberspace? Can Internet users demand respect from companies and governments?

Teachers can help students develop important twenty-first-century coping skills, such as making better online choices and gaining more control over their personal data. When it comes to basic subject matter, the challenge for today's teachers is how to motivate students for lifelong learning—while awakening curiosity and encouraging creativity.

In the last century, teachers emphasized the memorization of facts and answering questions correctly. Today, more attention is paid to helping students learn how science and mathematics relate to social problems, technology, creative innovation, and their personal lives (Peters and Stout, 2011).

A new pattern is emerging for teaching science and mathematics that attends to the content and characteristics of effective instruction. Engaging students in active and interactive learning deepens involvement in their academic work and understanding of the subjects we teach. Good teachers know that students should have many opportunities to interpret science and math ideas and arrive at understandings for themselves.

The latest approaches to science and math teaching encourage making an effort to be purposeful and providing students with meaningful activities with real applications that touch people's lives. By emphasizing collaborative inquiry, promoting curiosity, and valuing students' ideas, teachers can make these subjects more accessible and interesting.

A COLLABORATIVE MODEL FOR TEACHING SCIENCE AND MATH

Views of learning emphasize thinking processes within the learner and point toward changes that need to be made in the way that educators have traditionally thought about teaching, learning, and organizing the classroom. Central to creating such a learning environment is the desire to help individuals acquire or construct knowledge.

That knowledge is to be shared or developed—rather than held by the authority. It holds teachers to a high standard, for they must have both subject matter knowledge and pedagogical knowledge based on an understanding of learning and child development.

The collaborative learning model for inquiry in science and math emphasizes the intrinsic benefits of learning rather than external rewards for academic performance. Lessons are introduced with statements concerning reasons for engaging in the learning task. Students are encouraged to assume responsibility for learning and evaluating their own work and the work of others. Interaction may include a discussion of the validity of explanations, the search for more information, the testing of various explanations, or consideration of the pros and cons of specific decisions.

The characteristics that distinguish new collaborative science and mathematics learning revolve around group goals and the accompanying benefits of active group work. Instead of being told they need information, students learn to recognize when additional data is needed. They jointly seek it out, apply it, and see its power and value. In this way, the actual use of science and math information becomes the starting point rather than being viewed as an add-on. The teacher facilitates the process instead of acting as a knowledge dispenser. Student success is measured by performance, work samples, projects, and applications.

Scientific reasoning involves testing ideas through experimentation and a creative search for new ideas and applications.

Learning science and math in today's schools has a lot to do with exploring a problem, thinking, and posing a solution. This involves peers' helping one another, self-evaluation, and group support for risk taking. This also means accepting individual differences and having positive expectations for everyone in the group. When students understand the purpose of their tasks as contributing to their own learning, the process can help both the individual and the group.

If the teacher can help children push these elements together, the result will be greater persistence and more self-directed learning.

Making sure that there is plenty of time for active collaborative learning allows students to jointly address common topics at many levels of sophistication. This instructional method commonly involves having all students work on the same topic during a given unit. The work is divided into a number of investigatory or practical activities in which the students move from working alone to working in small groups.

Differentiated activities are organized to include basic required work and optional enrichment work. This way the groups that move more slowly should accomplish the basic requirements and still be able to choose some of the options. The more able groups should move on to more challenging assignments after completing the basic tasks. Because topics are not sequenced linearly, each new topic may be addressed, and differentiated instruction provided for.

IMPROVING TEACHING AND LEARNING

A constructive, active set of methods reflects the way science and math should be taught in the twenty-first century. The implication here is that classroom learning experiences should stimulate learners, build on past understandings, and encourage an exploration of the students' own ideas. The comprehension process is helped along when students are given multiple chances to interpret concepts and construct understandings for themselves.

The human brain has the ability to scan a vast warehouse of information, knowledge, and past experience to come up with unique solutions to problems. For many problems on the horizon, it is important to remember that solutions often take longer than you thought they would—and change happens faster than you thought it could.

Thinking and reasoning in science and math today have a lot to do with how things turn out in the future. Energizing students in a way that helps them grow into participants in tomorrow's social and technological changes requires engaging them in problem-solving investigations and projects today (Lannin, Ellis, Elliot, and Zbiek, 2011).

One of the good approaches to teaching math and science involves working with a partner for feedback on written work that relates to how problems were solved. To encourage peer review and joint authorship, we suggest that students keep daily logs or journal. As students talk together, they can better understand what they have been working on (before presenting their understandings in a group situation).

With the renewed emphasis on thinking, communicating, and making connections between topics, students are more in control of their learning. With collaborative inquiry, an important twenty-first-century skill, students gain many experiences with manipulatives, calculators, computers, and working on real-world applications.

There are more opportunities to make connections and work with peers on interesting problems. The ability to express basic math and science understandings, estimate confidently, and check the reasonableness of one's estimates are part of what it means to be literate, numerate, and employable.

OVERVIEW OF THE INTEGRATED SCIENCE AND MATH STANDARDS

All students should:

- Understand numbers and operations and estimate and use computational tools effectively

- Understand science and math subject matter, including physical, life, and earth/space science, algebra, and geometry
- Understand and use various patterns and relationships
- Use observation and special reasoning to solve problems
- Understand the themes and processes of science and mathematics
- Understand and use systems of measurement
- Become familiar with inquiry skills (pose questions, organize, and represent data)
- Focus on problem solving
- Recognize reasoning and proof as essential and powerful parts of science and mathematics
- Communicate ideas clearly to others by organizing and using thinking skills
- Understand the relationship of science, math, and technology and make connections among them
- Identify with the history, culture, and nature of science and mathematics
- Understand and practice science and mathematics from both personal and social perspectives

These selected integrated standards are derived from the National Science Education Standards (National Academy Press, 2011) and the Curriculum and Evaluation Standards for School Mathematics (National Council of Teachers of Mathematics, 2000).

SAMPLE ACTIVITIES

In an effort to link the integrated standards to classroom practice, a few sample activities are presented. The intent here is to present activities that could be modified and used in many grades, rather than to prescribe an activity for a unique grade level.

Activity 1: Compare and Estimate

Objectives

In grades K–4, the curriculum should include estimation so students can:

- Explore estimation strategies
- Recognize when an estimate is appropriate
- Determine the reasonableness of results
- Apply estimation in working with quantities and when using measurement, computation, and problem solving

Science and math instruction in the primary grades tries to make classifying and using numerals essential parts of the classroom experience. Students need to go beyond counting and writing numerals to identifying quantities and seeing relationships between objects.

When developing beginning concepts, learners need to manipulate concrete materials and relate numbers to problem situations. They benefit by talking, writing, and hearing what others think. In the following activity, students are actively involved in estimating, manipulating objects, counting, verbalizing, writing, and comparing.

Directions

1. Divide students into small groups of two or three. Place a similar set of color-coded objects in a container for each group. Pass out recording sheets divided into partitions with the color of the container in each box.
2. Have young students examine the container on their desks, estimate how many objects are present, discuss with their group, and write their guess next to the color on the sheet.
3. Next, have the group count the objects and write the number they counted next to the first number. Instruct the students to circle the greater number.
4. Switch containers or move to the next station and repeat the process. A variety of objects (small plastic cats, marbles, paper clips, colored shells, etc.) add interest and are real motivators.

Activity 2: Adding and Subtracting in Real-Life Situations

Objectives

In early grades, the science and mathematics curriculum should include concepts of addition and subtraction of whole numbers so that students can:

- Develop meaning for the operations by modeling and discussing a rich variety of problem situations
- Relate the mathematical language and symbolism of operations to problem situations and informal language

When children are learning about the operations of addition and subtraction, it's helpful for them to make connections between these processes and the world around them. Story problems using ideas from science help them see the actions of joining and separating. Using manipulatives and sample word problems gives them experiences in joining sets and figuring the differences between them. Pretending and using concrete materials makes learning more meaningful.

Directions

1. Divide students into small groups (two or three).
2. Tell stories in which the children can pretend to be animals, plants, other children, or even space creatures.
3. Telling stories is enhanced by having children use Unifix cubes or other manipulatives to represent the people, objects, or animals in the oral problems.
4. Have children work on construction paper or have them prepare counting boards where they draw things like trees, oceans, trails, houses, space stations, and so on.

Activity 3: Solving Problems

Problem solving should be the starting place for developing understanding. Teachers should present word problems for children to discuss and find solutions by working together, without the distraction of symbols. The following activities attempt to link word problems to meaningful situations:

Objectives

Students will:

- Solve problems
- Work in a group
- Discuss and present their solutions

Directions:

1. Divide students into small groups (two or three).
2. Find a creative way to share 50¢ among four children. Have them explain their solution. Is their solution fair? How would they do it differently?
3. Have the children in your class count and discover that there are 163 sheets of construction paper available. Have them figure out how many sheets each child would receive if the sheets were distributed evenly among them.
4. Encourage students to explain their reasoning to the class.
5. After discussing each problem, show the children the standard notation for representing division. Soon, you will find students that will begin to use the standard symbols in their own writing.

Activity 4: Using Statistics: Supermarket Shopping

Statistics is the science or study of data. Statistical problems require collecting, sorting, representing, analyzing, and interpreting information.

Objectives

Students will:

- Collect, organize, and describe data
- Construct, read, and interpret displays of data
- Formulate and solve problems that involve collecting and analyzing data

Problem:

1. Your group has $2.00 to spend at the market. What will you purchase?
2. Have groups explain and write down their choices.
3. Next, have groups collect data from all the groups in the class.
4. Graph the class results.

MAKING INTERDISCIPLINARY CONNECTIONS

Mathematics and technology have always served as important tools for work in the sciences. All three have major roles to play across the curriculum (Schwartz, 2008).

Science and math inform everything from history to the evening news. They enrich the visual and performing arts as well as sports and physical education. As an extension of our natural language, they provide a context for language learning.

As science and mathematics continue to become more integrated into society, their interconnectedness with other school subjects becomes an important goal (Burns, 2007).

INTERDISCIPLINARY MATH AND SCIENCE ACTIVITIES

It is best to get away from the idea of splitting up the curriculum— instead, the new focus is to fuse various disciplines together. The next few activities try to accomplish this goal.

Activity 5: Using the Sun to Teach Geometry

Objectives

Students will:

- Describe, model, draw, and classify shapes
- Investigate and predict the results of combining, subdividing, and changing shapes

- Develop spatial sense
- Relate geometric ideas to number and measurement ideas
- Recognize and appreciate geometry in their world

Directions

1. Have students investigate figures and their properties through shadow geometry, exploring what happens to shapes held in front of a point of light. They can also explore what happens to shapes held in the sunlight when the sun's rays are nearly parallel.
2. Have children discover which characteristics of the shapes are maintained under varying conditions. For this activity, provide pairs of children with square objects such as wooden or plastic squares.
3. Take students to an area of the playground that has a flat surface. Have the children hold the square objects so that shadows are cast on the ground. Encourage the children to move the square objects so that the shadows change.
4. Have students talk about the shadows they found. Discuss how they were able to make the shapes larger and smaller. See what other observations they have made.
5. To make a permanent record of shapes, have a student draw a shape on a piece of paper and put the piece of paper on the ground. Let the shadow fall on the paper. Have that student draw around the outline of the shadow.
6. When each student has had a chance to draw a favorite shape, there will be a collection of interesting drawings that can serve as a source for discussion, sorting, and display.
7. For a challenge activity: Students may also wish to discover if they can make a triangle or a pentagon shadow using the square object. Using outlines children drew of the shadows cast by square shapes, see if students can find things that are alike and different in the drawings.
8. Have students count the number of corners and sides of each shape and compare those numbers. Encourage them to discuss and record their conclusions.

Precaution

Be sure you direct students not to look at the sun directly.

Activity 6: Creating Maps

Objectives

Students will:

- Recognize, describe, extend, and create a wide variety of patterns
- Represent and describe math and science relationships
- Explore the use of variables and open sentences to express relationships

As students measure many geometric figures, they uncover patterns and see relationships. After students have explored different shapes, the next part of the activity looks at patterns. The topic is called *map making*. A map is a pattern that we follow. It tells us where to go and how we go about getting there. The following activity has students follow a map, recording as they go.

Directions

1. Have children use graph paper and a pencil to draw a path. Each unit on the grid will represent one city block.
2. Write the labels for north, east, south, and west. Begin your map in the middle of the graph paper. Then follow this route.

   a. Walk two blocks south.
   b. Turn east and walk three blocks.
   c. Turn south and walk one block.
   d. Turn east and walk three blocks.
   e. Turn south and walk four blocks.
   f. Turn east and walk one block.
   g. Turn south and walk three blocks.
   h. Turn west and walk half a block.

3. Compare your map to those of other students. How are they the same? How are they different? How would the map change if step B were a 90-degree turn west?
4. As a challenge problem: With your group, make a scale model of the local area. Include a "key" identifying symbols and directions.

Activity 7: Estimate and Weigh Different Materials

Objectives

Students will:

- Estimate the weight of different objects
- Relate everyday experiences to the math/science measuring activity

- Check their estimates

Children establish a link between their concrete everyday experience and their understanding of math and science abstractions through many different experiences in representing quantities and shapes. Representation helps children remember an experience and make sense by communicating it to others.

Directions

1. Fill several milk cartons with different materials such as rice, beans, clay, plaster of Paris, and wooden objects.
2. Seal the cartons and label them by color or letter. Tell the children what the materials are but do not identify the contents of a particular carton.
3. Have the children guess how to order the cartons by weight according to what they contain. Then, let the children order the cartons by weight, holding them in their hands and using the pan balance to check their estimates.

Activity 8: Which Will Melt More Quickly?

Objectives

Students will:

- Explore reasoning in science and mathematics
- Measure and compare quantities
- Write about their findings in their science and math journals

Problem

Suppose you have a glass of water. It has the same temperature as the air. Would an ice cube melt faster in the water or air? Invite students to find out.

Materials

Thermometer, water, ice cubes, two glasses (same), small plastic bag, salt, spoon.

Directions

1. Fill one container with warm water and leave the other container empty.

2. Let the children see and fill the cups with water. Explain, "We are going to put an ice cube in each container. Our problem: Which ice cube do you think will melt first? Write the guesses on the board."
3. Have students measure the temperature inside the empty glass. Also measure the temperature inside a glass of water. It should be about the same as the air temperature. If it is not, let the water stand a while.
4. Find two ice cubes of about the same size.
5. Put one cube into the empty glass. Put the other in the glass of water.
6. Compare how fast the ice cubes melt.

Questions for Further Investigation

1. How can you make an ice cube melt faster in water? Will stirring the water make a difference? Will it melt faster in warmer water? Does crushing the ice make a difference? Does changing the volume of the water matter?
2. How will ice cubes melt when other things are added to the water?
3. Will an ice cube melt faster in salt water? Does the amount of salt make a difference?
4. Students will measure and compare temperatures, hypothesize, experiment, and arrive at conclusions.

Evaluation

Have students explain their reasoning through writing about their experiment in their journals. Direct their discussion by asking them to explain what mathematics they used. What science skills were involved? What is the best way to show their data?

Activity 9: Science and Math Metric Challenge

Objectives

Students will:

- Solve problems through working as a team
- Explain directions

Directions

1. Divide the class into teams of three or four students.
2. Give each team a list of challenges:

- Find how many square meters of floor space each person in your classroom has.

- If there are 100 students in the gym, how many cubic meters does each student have?
- How many square meters does the school playground have?
- Find the number of meters you must walk from our classroom to the principal's office and back.
- Create a game with your group involving meters. Establish rules. Is luck involved? Write out the rules. Explain to the class how to play the game.

Activity 10: Design an Escher-Type Art Drawing

Students will become aware of the properties of shapes through many experiences. They will manipulate, visualize, draw, construct, and represent shapes in a variety of interesting, creative ways.

Objectives

Students will:

- Create patterns
- Explain their designs

Directions

1. Introduce the idea of making a repeated pattern (tessellation). Teachers may wish to talk about artists who use the concept of tessellation in their artwork.
2. Have students represent a three-dimensional object on paper.
3. Ask students what shapes can be seen in different objects.
4. Have them try to make a symmetrical design. What shapes will tile a floor (or tessellation)?
5. Begin by having students make a tessellated design. Encourage students to explain their pattern and the relationships between the figures they've chosen. Students who are adept at tessellating (drawing repeated patterns) may wish to extend that skill in artwork designs.

Through direct experiences with three-dimensional objects and then transferring those objects into a two-dimensional world, students become aware of the relationships and properties of geometric shapes. They will be able to notice symmetry in the designs they create. They will investigate how patterns look if they're moved or rotated. They draw, build, and describe many shapes from a variety of perspectives.

Activity 11: How Long Are You?

Objectives

Students will:

- Collect, organize, and describe data
- Measure and compare you and your partner's body parts
- Explain your measurements

1. With a partner, measure and compare the following body parts:

	You		*Partner*	
	Inches	Feet	Inches	Feet
a) Head to toe:	_____	____	_____	____
b) Arm span: fingertip to fingertip:	_____	____	_____	____
c) Forearm:	_____	____	_____	____
d) Foot:	_____	____	_____	____
e) Circumference around head:	_____	____	_____	____
f) Hand (pinky to thumb):	_____	____	_____	____

2. Explain your measuring technique and state your measurements.
3. Artwork: draw yourself and your partner's measurements and color.
4. Comparison sentences: What did you learn? _____
   _____
5. Share with the rest of the class.

Activity 12: Finding Your Heart Rate

Objectives

Students will:

- Understand the heart and its system
- Learn how to calculate their heart rate
- Understand that heart rate changes depend on physical activity
- Chart heart rate data

Materials

Classroom with room to move around, "calculate your heart rate" worksheet, pencils, timer or clock

Background Information

The heart is a pump. The heart pumps blood to parts of our body. The number of times the heart pumps per minute is called *heart rate*. Heart rate changes when we do different activities.

Procedures

Introduce the heart rate concept and have students guess how many beats per minute their heart is beating. Ask students to name activities they believe would change heart rate. Then, ask if they think these activities would make the heart beat faster or slower than normal. Explain to students that there are two main areas on the body where it is easiest to find your heart rate (neck and wrist). Have students find their pulse. Make sure each student has found it. Practice counting while being timed for ten seconds.

Directions

1. Pass out the heart rate worksheet. Have students calculate their heart rate while sitting.
2. Have students enter the number on the heart rate chart. Explain to students that this is how many times the heart beats in ten seconds.
3. Explain that heart rate is taken in one-minute intervals. Help students multiply their number by six in order to reach the number of times their heart beats in one minute. Enter the number on the worksheet.
4. Do the same for activities of standing and running in place for thirty seconds.
5. After the worksheet chart is filled in, ask students to write a sentence about a time when they felt their heart rate change.

Evaluation

Student performance will be evaluated according to how much of the chart they are able to fill in and how well they participated in the activity.

Heart Rate Worksheet

Your heart rate is how many times your heart beats per minute.
Your heart rate changes.
Your heart rate is your pulse.
Your pulse is found in your neck and wrist.

Record your heart rate below:

	Sitting	Standing	Running in Place
10 seconds	_____	_____	_____
	_____	_____	_____
60 seconds	_____	_____	_____
	_____	_____	_____

A useful instructional procedure: determine the purpose and scope of the lesson. Next: build on student interests as you provide space for thinking, reflection, and discussion. Be prepared to push student thinking forward with purposeful activities. Finally, share some of your lessons with other teachers and solicit suggestions for improvement.

Whether it is for individual or group work, it also makes sense for inquiry, scientific reasoning, and mathematical problem-solving skills to be integrated and utilized across the curriculum.

A SAMPLE OF ONLINE RESOURCES FOR STEM

Connected science, technology, engineering, and math (STEM) activities and projects are part of today's science and mathematics curriculum. The learning process associated with STEM views science and math as underlying all engineering problems. Technology is viewed as an essential tool in the search for answers.

Organizations like the National Science Teachers Association (www.nsta.org) and the National Council of Teachers of Mathematics (www.nctm.org) can help. So can the following Web sites:

- *AAAS Science NetLinks (http://sciencenetlinks.com)*
  The American Association for the Advancement of Science has made available a wide range of lesson plans for just about every grade level.
- *Discovery Education (www.discoveryeducation.com/teachers)*
  Here the content fits in nicely with state standards, and there are links to a large number of teacher-friendly math websites.
- *National Science Digital Library's K–6 Science Refreshers (http://nsdl.org/refreshers/science)*
  This site gives teachers a quick review of science concepts before they have to teach them. Also, there is a wide range of short lessons—covering everything from symbiosis and simple machines to weather forecasting.

- *PBS Teachers STEM Education Resource Center (www.pbs.org/teachers/ stem)*

  Here teachers and students can choose from thousands of resources—including lesson plans, videos, and interactive activities.
- *NASA's Planet Quest Exoplanet Exploration (http://exep.jpl.nasa.gov)*

  If students or teachers want to connect to experts, this is a good place to do it. Possibilities range from NASA's Jet Propulsion Laboratory (JPL) and images from space to the "Ask an Astronomer" podcast. Other possibilities: online games, activities, and submitting questions to experts.

All the sites referred to here invite curiosity in a way that stretches students' minds. Some of the visuals instill a sense of wonder, while many of the activities engage learners in a way that helps them ask insightful questions.

TEAMWORK AND INDIVIDUAL INQUIRY

The ability to work in small groups is an important twenty-first-century skill that reaches across the curriculum. Being able to function as part of a team is something that is important at any age. This is as true in math and science as anywhere else. In the world outside school, projects that rely on science and math often build on different points of view within the group to produce a coherent whole (Eichinger, 2004).

What about personal temperament and cultural imperatives? The cultural milieu we find ourselves in offers us templates, while leaving plenty of room for a variety of choices. Culture and psyche contribute to each other. In other words, both the culture and the individual's personality have a lot to do with how things get done. We shape our cultural templates and they shape us (Shweder, 1991).

In and out of school, groups functioning as a team sometimes encourage more persistence when it comes to working through a problem in today's diverse classrooms. As a consequence of group work, individuals can often be more motivated. The end result is often more enthusiasm and success for everyone.

Most tasks can be made more interesting by making at least some space for a team approach. Small cooperative groups can handle more sophisticated problems than individuals working alone. Organizing students in a way that leaves space for both individual and group work allows teachers to channel energy into productive communication and problem solving. Such an arrangement also gives students an opportunity to take more responsibility for their own learning. Of course, there is no freedom in a vacuum.

Even when students are working in small groups, the teacher guides, mentors, and advises. It is, after all, the teacher who sets up groups and encourages everybody to take responsibility for themselves and for other team members. An example from mathematics instruction: a good approach is to set up situations where student groups can develop math arguments that are based on representations and then go on to describe consistencies across problems (Russell, Schifter, and Bastable, 2012).

When students focus on their own investigations, discussions, and group projects, the teacher's role shifts from chalk-and-talk to expert manager. The whole-class setting can be used for initial brainstorming, giving directions, summarizing data, reviewing different strategies, and arriving at common understandings about the questions that come up. From time to time, the whole class can come together for a brief explanation of group work.

To prepare for an uncertain future, it is important for teachers to raise provocative questions. At the same time, it also makes sense to encourage students to use what they have learned to illuminate a new phenomenon.

A good teacher knows how to ask the right question in different situations. Some of these questions can be worked on alone, then discussed in small groups, and finally, brought up with the entire class. Teachers may also want to use the larger class setting to summarize and highlight important ideas that come from the work of the small groups (Wetzel, 2012).

At some point, it is important for both individuals and learning teams to move from freewheeling idea creation to sorting the good ideas from the bad. Working with one, two, or three peers can help diminish some of the fear surrounding science and math and amplify student understanding. Small collaborative groups can also help generate an appreciation for the power and beauty of science and mathematics.

Call it collaborative, cooperative, or team learning; the essential point is that strategies for teaching science and mathematics that involve social interaction result in children's gaining more control of the math and science curriculum. This includes the need for individual students to ask the hard questions and take risks in a supportive community (Wedekind, 2011).

CHALLENGING SCIENCE AND MATH ACTIVITIES

The next section brings together the science and math standards to elementary and middle school classrooms. Meaningful activities that employ the core ideas and practices of observing, comparing, measuring, recording data, and making good conclusions are emphasized. These activities are based on the 2010 National Framework for K–12 Science Education Standards. Whenever possible, the Mathematics Standards (2011) are included.

Activity 1: Mysterious Stories

Stories are a means of communication. Even before written language, people drew pictures on the walls of their caves to show a successful hunt or the animals they met. Stories can include rules and accomplishments found in everything from dance to pictures, visual arts, and words.

It is important to view stories as a desire for people to communicate their thoughts, dreams, and mysteries across generations. Looking at stories as mysteries is exciting, and it provides students with characters they can identify with and allows them to be included and be part of the adventure.

Activity 2: Invent a Mystery Story

Create your own mystery story.

Activity 3: The Mystery of Gravity and Yo-Yos

Content Standards

- Applying the core ideas of physical science
- Comparing movement and gravity

Objectives

- Students observe objects concerning force, acceleration, friction, and gravity. Students apply physics to real-world situations.

Background Information

Students should review the basic physics principles of gravity and inertia.

- Gravity: a natural force of attraction that tends to draw objects together
- Inertia: a property of matter whereby it remains at rest or continues in uniform motion unless attracted by some outside force
- Velocity: rate of change of position

Questions

How do yo-yos reflect physics?
What is an example of inertia?
How does your yo-yo show force?
Can you make your yo-yo accelerate?
What causes friction when using a yo-yo?
Can you explain why a yo-yo shows gravity?

Other Student Activities

Students work in pairs with the yo-yos.

1. Estimate the direction your yo-yos moved in one minute.
2. Record the velocity of your yo-yos. What speed do you think they traveled?
3. Write a mystery story about your yo-yos and how they demonstrate gravity.
4. Why does a yo-yo act as it does?
5. There are some professional yo-yo groups. Find out more about them. Record your findings.

Activities for Accelerated Students

1. Slow down your yo-yo, then try to speed it up.
2. What happens when the yo-yo is thrown in a different direction?
3. What makes the yo-yo slow down?
4. When does the yo-yo move fast?
5. Describe the physics involved in these activities.
6. Record your yo-yo's movements. Compare them with those of other students.
7. With other students, describe the force, speed, gravity, and friction of your yo-yos. Record your findings.
8. Make a class chart so other classes can see your physical science achievements.

Activity 4: Flowing Mysteries

Content Standards

- Applying the physical science standards
- Using basic ideas and procedures in science
- Putting personal views to practical use
- Practicing oral and written communication skills
- Employing science and technology skills

Materials

Students are experimenting with household chemicals
Student tools for each workstation:

6 small plastic bottles
6 flowing substances (vinegar, soap, alcohol, cooking oil, vanilla, water)
6 short glass tubes with rubber bulb
1 wide-mouthed drinking cup

1 small drinking cup
1 flat-bottomed container for holding articles
1 piece of saran wrap
1 sheet of aluminum foil
1 sheet of waxed paper
1 sheet of white paper
food coloring

Directions

1. Prepare the containers with food coloring added.
2. Have students discuss how scientists perform experiments.
3. Prepare the trays and tools for each group.
4. On the chalkboard, list the experiments that students might try:

- Substance races
- Floating ability
- Density
- Combining liquids
- Other suggestions

Student Task

Discover which of the six chemicals are observing the following rules:

- Use your sense of sight to find out what the flowing mysteries are.
- You are not to smell, touch, or taste the chemicals.
- Each dropper can be used to pick up only one substance.

Students rotate among the workstations, experimenting as they try to discover what the flowing mysteries are. They conduct several tests during the process.

Workstation 1: Substance Races

Lesson Steps

1. Choose a substance and a sheet of paper to cover your tray (waxed paper, white paper, aluminum foil, saran wrap).
2. Place a drop of each substance on the paper.
3. Tip the tray so the substance moves.
4. Record the movement of the chemicals.
5. Try the experiment with all the flowing chemicals.

Workstation 2: Floating Ability

Lesson Steps

1. Select a small plastic container.
2. Add drops of each colored substance.
3. We want to see which substances will float.
4. Encourage students to experiment.
5. Jerk, shake, and maneuver the container to detect which chemicals move to the top.
6. Record the movement of the chemicals.

Workstation 3: Density

Lesson Steps

1. Select a small plastic container.
2. Add drops of each colored substance.
3. We want to see which substances will sink.
4. Encourage students to experiment.
5. Jerk, shake, and maneuver the container to detect which chemicals sink.
6. Record the movement of the chemicals.

Workstation 4: Combining Liquids

Lesson Steps

1. Guess what each substance is and test your guesses by observing which substances blend together.
2. Record your guesses

- blue chemical _____
- green chemical _____
- red chemical _____
- yellow chemical _____
- purple chemical _____
- clear chemical _____
- Which will mix? Write your reasoning:
- oil _____
- soap _____
- water _____
- vanilla _____
- vinegar _____
- alcohol _____

CONNECTING THE MATH STANDARDS TO THE CORE CONTENT STANDARDS

Standard 1: Understand Numbers and Operations

Students need to understand counting (represent one-to-one correspondence with concrete materials; match a set to a numeral).

Standard 2: Ability to Use Patterns, Algebra, Functions, and Variables

Students will understand and use functions (plus +, minus -, times x, divide /).

Standard 3: Geometry

Apply geometry, understand shapes, and use size, symmetry, congruence, and similarity.

Standard 4: Measurement

Use measurement to measure and compare lengths and widths; tell and write time in hours and half hours; and use analog and digital clocks.

Standard 5: Data Analysis, Probability

Organize data; use charts, tables, graphs, and statistics to make sense of mathematics.

Standard 6: Problem Solving

Find solutions, use strategies, take risks, make decisions, and get results.

Standard 7: Reasoning

Reasoning is connected to students' language development. Thinking and reasoning are important to math learning. Students should have experiences with deductive reasoning (moving from guesses to conclusions).

Learners should also be aware of inductive reasoning (informal reasoning using specific examples) and use evidence to make assumptions and form conclusions.

Standard 8: Communicating

This includes working in groups, talking, listening, and expressing ideas. Students share information, explain ideas, and help each other.

Standard 9: Forming Conclusions

Many relationships are learned every day by students making connections through their own experiences and applying math content to real-life situations.

Standard 10: Representing Math Relationships

Using or representing 0 (zero) involves showing connections among math concepts and improves understanding. Particularly in the elementary grades, learning becomes more enjoyable when students are able to use different blocks, colored math squares, and fraction pieces while performing math skills.

CAPTURING STUDENT INTEREST/ENGAGED LEARNING

It makes sense to emphasize cognitively challenging and developmentally appropriate activities. In the primary grades, it is especially important that children begin to have science/math experiences involving the exploratory use of materials, open-ended discussions, dramatic play, music, and art.

Making connections with other disciplines and real-world concerns energizes both students and their teachers. It also helps make science and math more meaningful—a key to making sense of these subjects and capturing student interest (Small, 2008).

Ask students to draw a scientist or mathematician. Chances are you will get a picture of an older man with wild hair, glasses, and a white lab coat. To show how wrong these preconceived stereotypes are, have students go to the Tumblr Web site "This Is What a Scientist Looks Like." (Scientists from all over the world have posted pictures of themselves with a brief description about who they are.)

Student learning teams are a powerful way to undo preconceived notions about science and math. To help students achieve a deeper understanding, more attention is being given to application and social interaction. Clearly, collaborative inquiry and problem-solving activities are important routes to deeper understandings of science and mathematics (Jadrich and Bruxvoort, 2011).

The best academic mix of individual and group work has a lot to do with a person's preferred social style (Cain, 2012). So for some students, it may sometimes be best to begin a lesson by encouraging them to individually embrace the power of reflective thinking. The first step might be working alone for a while. Next, have the students discuss their thoughts with a partner; then, move on to a group of three or four.

Small groups work well in the classroom. Being socially connected can turn into a wasteful distraction from real experiences. But on- or off-line, nonstop socializing can be a distraction. It almost seems as though some people just can't stop talking or texting. *Individual* experience, playfulness, spontaneity, and intellectual curiosity still matter, however. And leaving a little space and quiet time for personal reflection may help encourage independent thinking.

TEAMWORK, REFLECTION, AND MOVING THE FURNITURE

In tomorrow's classrooms, interactive learning by small groups of students will be the norm. This makes sense because peer support helps learners feel more confident and willing to make mistakes and engage in scientific inquiry and problem solving in mathematics. Collaboration, in concert with a little human friction, has a lot to do with how scientists and mathematicians advance their fields.

Criticism and debate do not necessarily inhibit imaginative thinking or innovation. In fact, informed criticism can actually encourage people to dig deeper and come up with more useful and fewer predictable ideas. After all, not every new idea is necessarily useful or equally worthy of praise. In fact, false praise actually has a negative effect on the quality of a student's imaginative work.

With any subject or topic, a brainstorming or freewheeling approach is fine—just leave a little space for collaborative evaluation. For example, when it comes to the technological products of science and mathematics, it is important to question the significance of things like the Internet, social networks, and collaborative computer games.

Try asking students to explain the ideas that drive their work, the hypothesis they generate from those ideas, and why their conclusions make sense. This kind of circular thought/discussion process is likely to result in a deeper understanding of what is being studied.

Essential twenty-first-century skills include thinking abstractly, communicating, and working with others. Also included are the abilities to work with numbers, read text, use computers, and learn new material.

Whatever the topic, at some point, students must learn to pool their creative thoughts and figure out how to put what they have learned into practice. With some topics, there is very little that is completely new, and often, the most imaginative thing to do is to figure out new ways of illuminating what is familiar.

The road to the future should be paved with the deepest wells of information. Exposure to other ways of thinking—and testing convictions against competing ways of viewing the world—has a lot to do with what education is all about.

It is always wise to encourage children and young adults to become familiar with a wide range of perspectives. The next step is moving on to draw imaginative conclusions that are based on what they have studied and what they believe.

Individual idea creation, critical thinking, teamwork, and debate surely will be part of any future science/math package. So, in the classroom get used to the furniture, the quiet spaces, the ideas, and the discussion getting moved around.

SUMMARY, CONCLUSION, AND LOOKING FORWARD

The insights of modern science have come about with the help of mathematics and technology. Combining these tools with the processes of scientific reasoning opens up possibilities for discoveries that lead to a better understanding of the world.

The imaginative implications of science, math, and their technological associates reach well beyond the schools. Mastering these subjects may not result in innovation, but they certainly increase the odds of it happening.

As far as mathematics instruction is concerned, teachers have to go beyond teaching students basic arithmetic, how to balance a checkbook, or how to estimate how long it will take to get from one town to another. Students should learn to ask the big questions—as they consider how math might be applied to broader human problems.

As far as specific classroom content is concerned, it is not enough to teach computation and procedures in isolation from the situations that require those skills. Those who teach science and mathematics also have a responsibility to meet the challenges of technology and society.

To thrive in a creative way in the classroom, it helps if students can see the unique work of others. And they need to be in an environment where imaginative work is valued. Cognitive capacity and subject-matter knowledge matter, but creative individuals tend to have a risk-taking personality and temperament. Still, like the idea of multiple intelligences, there are many different kinds of creativity—and there are multiple paths to imaginative ideas (Sinclair, 2006).

Whatever approach you take in incorporating creativity into your lessons, it is important to remember that failure is widely recognized as part of the creative process (Carson, 2010). (It certainly helps if you know how to learn from false starts and mistakes.) We all know that not every idea generated is going to be a good idea. However, the more new ideas that are produced, the more likely it is that something unique and useful will turn up.

Being naive or afraid of science or mathematics can be a real problem in school, in the workplace, and for citizens in a democracy. The key to academic success in these subjects is fostering habits of the mind such as critical thinking, problem solving, agility, adaptability, curiosity, and imagination. In a world filled with the technological products of science and math understanding, these subjects are more important than ever.

Knowing how to use a wide range of scientific and mathematical tools to solve problems in an imaginative way is an essential skill for today's world. It is also important to have some idea of how science and math impact life on a daily basis. At any age, academic competency in science and math increasingly includes an understanding of the roles these subjects serve in society.

With today's digital media, such as the Internet, the ability to synthesize a wide range of inputs (while focusing on the big picture) matters more than ever. As a consequence, any list of twenty-first-century skills should include the ability to sort through a glut of information and quickly figure out what's useful.

The need for analytical skills and social intelligence goes with any version of the future. These skills have a lot to do with innovation. And it is innovation that carries us forward; rarely does it go backward. Still, in spite of certain agreed-on principles, uncertainty and change go with the territory.

A good way to get ready for the murky situations and big ideas that are just beyond the horizon is to look around today. Notice how the future often gets mashed up with the past.

In any discussion of the future, it is important to keep in mind the caution that history doesn't repeat; it rhymes.

> The future is already here. It's just not evenly distributed yet.
> —William Gibson

SUGGESTED RESOURCES

Esler, W., and M. Esler. (2001). *Teaching elementary science.* Belmont, CA: Wadsworth.

Etheredge, S., and A. Rudnitsky. (2003). *Introducing students to scientific inquiry: How do we know what we know?* Boston: Allyn & Bacon.

Kennedy, L., and S. Tipps. (2000). *Guiding children's learning of mathematics.* Belmont, CA: Wadsworth.

Krauss, L. (2012). *A universe from nothing: Why there is something rather than nothing.* New York: Free Press (Simon & Schuster).

Lowrey, L. F. (1997). *NSTA pathways to the science standards—elementary school edition.* Arlington, VA: NSTA Press (National Science Teachers Association).

National Council of Teachers of Mathematics (NCTM). (2000). *Principles and standards for school mathematics.* Reston, VA: National Council of Teachers of Mathematics.

National Research Council (NRC) (2001). *The national mathematics standards 2001.* Washington, DC: NRC.

Whitin, P., and D. Whitin. (2000). *Math is language too: Talking and writing in the mathematics classroom.* Reston, VA: National Council of Teachers of Mathematics. Urbana, IL: National Council of Teachers of English.

REFERENCES

Andrews, L. (2012). *I know who you are and I saw what you did*. New York: Free Press.

Bogan, L. (1980). *Journey around my room: The autobiography of Louis Bogan*. New York: Viking.

Brown, M. (2012). *Quotable Quotes about Math and Science*. Dallas: National Math and Science Initiative.

Burns, M. (2007). *About teaching mathematics: A K–8 resource*. Sausalito, CA: Math Solutions.

Bybee, R. (2010). *The teaching of science in the 21st century*. Arlington, VA: NSTA Press (National Science Teachers Association).

Cain, S. (2012). *Quiet: The power of introverts in a world that can't stop talking*. New York: Crown.

Carson, S. (2010). *Your creative brain: Seven steps to maximize imagination, productivity, and innovation in your life*. Hoboken, NJ: Wiley.

Dweck, C. (2006). *Mindset: The new psychology of success*. New York: Random House.

Eichinger, J. (2004). *40 strategies for integrating science and mathematics instruction: K–8*. Upper Saddle River, NJ: Prentice Hall.

Froschauer, L., and M. Bigelow. (2012). *Rise and shine: A practical guide for the beginning science teacher*. Arlington, VA: NSTA Press (National Science Teachers Association).

Gibson, W. (2012). *Distrust that particular flavor*. New York: G. P. Putnam's & Sons.

Jadrich, J., and C. Bruxvoort. (2011). *Learning and teaching scientific inquiry: Research and applications*. Arlington, VA: NSTA Press (National Science Teachers Association).

Lannin, J., A. Ellis, R. Elliot, and R. Zbiek. (2011). *Developing essential understanding of mathematical reasoning for teaching mathematics in grades pre-K–8*. Reston, VA: National Council of Teachers of Mathematics.

Leinwand, S. (2012). *Sensible mathematics: A guide for school leaders in the era of common core standards*. 2nd ed. Portsmouth, NH: Heinemann.

National Academy Press. (2011). *National science education standards*. Washington, DC: National Academy Press.

National Research Council (NRC). (2011). *A framework for K–12 science education: Practices, crosscutting concepts, and core ideas*. Washington, DC: NRC.

Neagoy, M. (2012). *Planting the seeds of algebra, pre-K–2: Explorations for the early grades*. Thousand Oaks, CA: Corwin.

Peters, J., and D. Stout. (2011). *Science in elementary education: Methods, concepts, and inquiries*. 11th ed. Boston: Allyn & Bacon.

Russell, S., D. Schifter, and V. Bastable. (2012). *Connecting arithmetic to algebra: Strategies for building algebraic thinking in the elementary grades*. Portsmouth, NH: Heinemann.

Schwartz, S. (2008). *Teaching young children mathematics*. Lanham, MD: Rowman & Littlefield.

Shweder, R. (1991). *Thinking through cultures*. Cambridge, MA: Harvard University Press.

Sinclair, N. (2006). *Mathematics and beauty: Aesthetic approaches to teaching children*. New York: Teachers College Press.

Small, M. (2008). *Making math meaningful to Canadian students, K–8*. Toronto, ON: Nelson Education.

Wedekind, K. (2011). *Math exchanges: Guiding young mathematicians in small group meetings*. Portland, ME: Stenhouse.

Wetzel, D. (2012). *Teaching science and math: Resources and strategies for K–12 science and math teachers*. Arlington, VA: NSTA Press (National Science Teachers Association).

SIX

Reading and Writing

Literacy and Language Skills in a Changing World

> Reading usually precedes writing and the impulse to write is fired by reading. I write to find out what I am thinking, looking at, and what it means. It isn't so much to solve problems as to let them emerge.
> —Anonymous

Reading and writing are fundamental building blocks of communication by which we live, learn, work, share, and build understandings. They cut across all subjects and are rooted in the oral language that is learned at home and at school. So it is little wonder that comprehending the printed word and being able to write remain central to language and literacy learning.

In addition to traditional literacy concerns, learning to understand and harness the power of today's visually intensive media is increasingly associated with the ability to read, write, and think critically. Of course, there is no guarantee that dizzying technological change will result in progress.

The creation of virtual worlds is no substitute for advances in the physical world. The computing and interconnected world may be helpful. But such tech tools will be useful only if they serve as a means to an end, rather than an end in themselves.

Successful language and literacy learning have a lot to do with a student's home environment and work at school. When it comes to specific methods for teaching reading and writing, it is important to remember that the goal is comprehension. Understanding what we read, for example, is based on being able to identify the letters and sounds that make up words, determining what the words mean, figuring out how the concepts fit together, and making inferences that go beyond the text.

Literacy learning involves acquiring skills and strategies for understanding, thinking about, and using information from what has been written. Whether it is language arts instruction, thinking skills, technology, or helping students prepare for an uncertain future, the enthusiasm and energy of the teacher are keys to academic success. The same principle applies to active parental support.

In the twenty-first century, "literacy" also intersects with understanding images, digital media, and emerging technologies. So it is little wonder that students are increasingly expected to be able to create and express themselves with print, sound, and images on a screen.

Schools have always been charged with making sure that students become knowledgeable and literate enough with the media of the day to eventually contribute to their culture and workplace. But it is important to remember that a quality educational system is also expected to inspire students and to expose them to new ideas and challenges.

LANGUAGE, LITERACY, AND THE SOCIAL NATURE OF LEARNING

A major goal of literacy instruction is to ensure that all students can read and write well enough to succeed in school and function as informed members of society. A wide range of reading-related learning is essential to a healthy democracy and meaningful civic engagement. Literacy skills are also essential for helping learners make meaning from the information in their lives and become familiar with the world around them (Shannon, 2011).

Language and literacy skills are central to pursuing individual and group interests at any age. In the early grades, the instructional focus is on learning to read and write; later, it's using these skills to learn about and appreciate a wide variety of subjects.

As far as digital technology is concerned, the results have been mixed. Computer-based reading and writing software may result in more engaged students and parents. But statistically significant instructional results from e-learning are proving to be hard to come by (Welner, Hinchey, and Molnar, 2010). Also, if students get too beguiled by mere gadgetry, they may miss more important aspects of what learning should be about.

It *is* clear that teachers can engage students and promote literacy in a variety of ways, including making use of small collaborative groups to accomplish instructional goals. As students learn to work together in small groups, they go beyond learning to manage their relationships to accomplish their academic goals.

Social media fundamentally changes the communications technology landscape. Some teachers find social media, like Facebook and Twitter, good at building and maintaining ties to friends, colleagues, and students. But many educators say that social media makes them feel more distant and alienated. Is there a middle ground that takes advantage of social media and protects users?

Many school districts are developing social media policies for teachers and students; some approach it as a useful educational tool, while others ban it altogether. If you do decide to try to use social media to communicate with students, Facebook has some suggestions on how to engage students while keeping a carefully defined professional barrier. One thing is for sure: it is best for teachers to keep work work and personal life personal.

The social context has a strong influence on literacy learning. With or without technology, students need to interact with others. And learners must build a solid foundation for expanding communication skills and comprehension processing abilities. Interpersonal skills go hand in hand with acquiring the additional language knowledge that is needed to support reading and writing development.

When it comes to innovation and creative outcomes, the imaginative processes that lead to inventive ideas must be at least partly out of control. Unpredictable outcomes can be valuable within the innovation process (Austin, Devin, and Sullivan, 2011). Also, important points like how expansive technological change can be may be obscured by a fascination with whiz-bang gadgets.

FUNDAMENTAL BUILDING BLOCKS OF CREATIVITY AND LITERACY

Having the ability to control and appreciate the reading and writing processes is a key variable in the inventive process. Teachers who construct environments that are conducive to creativity and innovation can steer literacy and knowledge in ways that facilitate valuable accidents. It also helps if you can encourage learners to get outside what they normally think of. Along the way, simulations and other possibilities associated with technology can support the development of inventive processes across the curriculum (Randall, 2011).

When it comes to reading and writing, group interaction, motivation, persistence, and the effective use of comprehension strategies all help. Print-to-meaning (word analysis knowledge) comes naturally to successful readers. Clearly, the ability to infer word and story meaning in light of background knowledge and instructional goals helps with comprehension.

If everything goes well, by the time students get to the upper elementary grades, young readers and writers will be automatically processing the skills needed to do productive work.

It seems likely that the nature of human learning will increasingly be explained by sciences of the mind, brain, and evolution. It is just as likely that knowledge about the structure of the brain will facilitate our understanding of the human mind *if* it is accompanied by sound theories of the mind, behavior, and learning.

When it comes to reading, writing, and cognitive development, politics often gets tangled with science. Across the curriculum, government guidelines sometimes try to build on the "science" from a few narrow studies that support a predetermined position.

When it comes to human intelligence and learning, certain discoveries about human nature have been ignored or suppressed. For example, controversy and negative accusations have surrounded anyone who has suggested that some aspects of language and literacy development might be molded by genes.

Equity and fairness do not depend on sameness. Human minds don't come into this world equally blank and free of innate, genetically shaped abilities and behaviors. There is general agreement that environmental infusion is necessary to activate or realize every biological trait. There is also agreement that most intellectual differences among the races are probably due to unequal experience. However, many of the cognitive traits distinguishing the sexes may be explained genetically.

When it comes to schooling, exemplary teachers are usually able to help every child move in the direction of reaching his or her unique potential. Good teachers build on each individual's abilities, while respecting a student's prior knowledge and cultural background. Culture, race, or a child's gender is never a good excuse for poor teaching.

Whatever innate behavioral differences exist between males and females, there is no reason why we can't teach boys to read and write as well as girls. Some teachers have found that graphic novels or comic books can sometimes enhance literacy learning. Whether it is reading, composing, or illustrating, narration boxes can provide background, setting, and plot information. Also, putting text in narration boxes can convey what the characters are saying and thinking in a way that motivates reluctant readers (Carter, 2007).

Certain text types (like nonfiction) and features like visuals are more likely to engage boys because of the way they encourage readers to connect to the world. Boys may respond best to interesting graphics and a chance to share their learning. It also helps if what they read is more closely connected to real life. In addition, boys seem to like knowing why they are reading—and they like being able to use what they read to talk, do, or make something.

BECOMING COMPETENT READERS, WRITERS, AND THINKERS

Whatever their background is and after a few years of schooling, good readers and writers have a literacy background that helps them comprehend word, sentence, and story structure. The social arrangements within which reading and writing occur go a long way toward explaining the academic and social outcomes for individuals.

Well-designed reading and writing activities build on each child's knowledge base and unique abilities. When individuals feel that they have information, resources, or skills that are needed by other group members, they are more likely to feel that successful group work is important to their personal achievement.

A POSITIVE INSTRUCTIONAL ENVIRONMENT

- Promotes cooperative investigation and active learning
- Involves predicting, questioning, and story sharing
- Includes high expectations with many opportunities to succeed
- Provides opportunities to observe, write, and use electronic media
- Generates ongoing feedback and authentic assessment

The real test is whether or not the student understands what's been taught and can apply it powerfully.

LITERACY ACROSS THE GRADE LEVELS

Literacy is more than just a set of skills for reading, writing, speaking, and viewing. It's a complex web of social activities for constructing meaning while communicating, comprehending, and producing. As a child's linguistic repertoire expands, literacy emerges as old patterns are refined and new ones added.

When they arrive at school, some children think that the meaning in a book resides in pictures, and others simply don't know what reading is about. Before too long, most realize that the printed language in a story is an important meaning source.

In the early grades, children learn about sound-symbol relationships, the importance of syllables, and concepts such as words and sentences. Rhyming stories, poems, and words can help students discriminate orally among the sounds of language.

Discriminating visually among letters and words will lead to using context clues to make meaning and follow the sequence of a story. As reading skills develop, children read at times with fluency, and at other times with miscues. As readers become more adept, they become better at predicting and self-correcting meaning inferred from text.

Most children quickly progress from reading pictures to independently reading text. This involves applying a wide range of strategies to comprehend, interpret, and appreciate the printed word. Deriving a social sense of what linguistic forms work in a particular social context goes hand in hand with the conventional reading of print.

By the time students get to the upper elementary grades, they realize that printed language is usually the principal meaning source in books, magazines, and newspapers. Students soon realize that reading and writing are fundamental vehicles for gaining new knowledge about all subjects. Successful readers and writers are able to apply these language skills across the curriculum—as they become reflective and knowledgeable members of a variety of literacy communities.

LANGUAGE, SOCIAL INTERACTION, AND AUTHENTIC ASSESSMENT

Language learning and associated concept development are motivated by mental maturation and by social interactions. Even understanding how language can serve as a representation of meaning is influenced by the social and communication experiences of children (Boyd and Galda, 2011).

Adult modeling always helps the reading and writing processes along. So does the opportunity to interact verbally with adults and peers. Background experiences, a solid literature base, and plenty of reader-writer transactions with text all matter. It is up to the teachers to take all of these into account as they organize the classroom, choose the instructional methods, and build on the characteristics of effective instruction.

Integrating the language arts is a powerful way to connect students to the full range of real communication possibilities. The children who are active in their own language and literacy development are more likely to gain control over word, sentence, and text structure. The process is very interactive. Once meaning construction is under way, the social nature of language learning becomes even more obvious.

To achieve reading comprehension and writing fluency, students need to:

- Understand the aesthetic elements of visual, oral, and written texts
- Communicate with printed, visual, auditory, and electronic media
- Think analytically and creatively about important themes and concepts
- Use communication skills to develop insights about human experiences

- Connect knowledge from all curriculum areas to understand the world

Reading and writing relate directly to each other and other language skills. Of course, the development of communication skills is much more than learning a specified set of subskills. Learning the English language arts involves becoming active, critical, and creative users of print, spoken language, and the visual language of film, television, and digital media.

Reading and other language skills are learned from parents, teachers, and peers in a social setting. Success is based on a combination of innate and learned traits.

Language and literacy learning, at their best, are a social activity with an academic focus. An important goal is to help children gain the ability to use language to communicate information, ideas, experiences, and feelings.

Meaningful group activities and settings can help students learn how to use language to communicate, solve problems, and meet the diverse literacy demands that they will encounter throughout their lives. Social interaction matters, but the key to high-quality language arts instruction is still the same: a language-rich classroom where the teacher understands the content and follows the basic principles of effective instruction.

As teachers look for new ways to make the language arts more active, dynamic, purposeful, and fun, it is important to recognize the importance of personal adaptability and creativity. In the current consumer-oriented, test-obsessed America of today, it is increasingly difficult to find the instructional space to be an inspiring or innovative teacher.

Assessment can be part of regular conversations with students about their work. If teachers are aware of their students' progress in relation to standards, the possibility of raising the bar opens up if students exceed expectations.

Assessment and standards can sometimes help, but rigid scripts designed by others are a poor substitute for well-educated teachers who can combine professional flexibility with the latest in good instructional technique. Good teachers are always looking at the work of their peers and assessing themselves. They notice if a student isn't learning and they evaluate students' work through portfolios, quizzes, tests, and a range of other performance measures.

Successful schools communicate clearly to teachers and students what quality of work is expected. But standards shouldn't result in standardization. Educators have to find ways to attend to outside pressures and still retain the capacity to release the creative power in the children they teach.

ESOL, ESL, AND ENGLISH PROFICIENCY

Over the last twenty years, the American student population has changed dramatically. In the last three decades, more people have immigrated to the United States and Canada than in the previous two hundred years. As far as the schools are concerned, the result is a student population with great diversity in language, culture, and achievement. The important unanswered question of the day is how much training, if any, should a child have in his or her first language if it is not English?

Whatever the fate of bilingual education, now (more than ever) teachers must understand the nature of language diversity. And they must be able to use instructional strategies that are effective in teaching a second language (i.e., English) to students. Attending to cultural differences goes beyond the English language arts. Today's teachers are often called on to provide instruction that satisfies specific cultural needs. They must also be able to help all students comprehend how different cultures have contributed to American society.

Ready or not, schools are being charged with ensuring the educational development of linguistically diverse populations. English for speakers of other languages (ESOL) and English as a second language (ESL) programs have become part of the educational landscape. A common goal of such programs is to help language minority students quickly attain proficiency in English in order to make satisfactory achievement in the regular school program. Fortunately, most of what works with limited English proficiency (LEP) students also works with all students.

Sample Strategies for Teaching ESOL Students

- Include ESOL students as part of regular classroom groups.
- Use mixed-ability cooperative and collaborative grouping arrangements.
- Give students opportunities to use their life experiences in assignments.
- Use graphic organizer strategies such as Venn diagrams and webbing.
- Use cloze strategies and language experience techniques in reading.
- Use peer tutors and check to see if everyone demonstrates understanding.
- Have students work with a partner to revise and edit written work.

A good ESOL curriculum provides for the development of communication skills in listening, speaking, reading, and writing. While attending to language diversity and bilingual skills, today's schools emphasize the development of competency in speaking, reading, writing, and understanding English. As students gain a reasonable command of basic functional vocabulary and grammatical structure, they become able to read, write, and use related language skills across the curriculum.

Early on, the teacher may have to adapt some assignments to meet the needs of ESOL students. But it shouldn't be long before these students are able to participate effectively in learning the same subject matter offered to all students.

Making classrooms inclusive and finding effective ways to teach a diverse group of students are part of quality teaching. Remember, reading and writing are major predictors of student performance across the curriculum. And those who have trouble with these subjects are more likely to drop out of school later on (Hall, Burns, and Edwards, 2011).

As a teacher, you must recognize that although your academic qualifications are important, your beliefs and attitudes will strongly influence your teaching. As with other aspects of teaching, knowledge, self-understanding, and reflection about intercultural interactions are essential for teachers in today's multicultural classrooms.

Students need to know that the heritage, culture, and language they bring to school are honored and respected (Schmidt and Lazar, 2011). Although children may possess a first language that is different from that of their teachers, it doesn't mean that those who use something other than standard English at home necessarily suffer from language deficits. Expert teachers understand this. They also know that a student's acquisition of language and literacy abilities is meaning based and best developed in an interactive, content-rich, and supportive classroom environment.

EMERGENT LITERACY

Emergent literacy is a continuum of understandings that gives children the ability to read, write, and use various communication tools. Within this context, literacy is viewed as a continuous process that begins during the first months of life and continues throughout life. (Although the whole range is important, here the focus is on elementary and middle grade learners.)

Interactive Digital Storybooks for Primary Grade Children?

Think about both sides of the argument:

On the plus side, it is important to get books into the hands of children; the delivery vehicle doesn't matter. The iPad, for example, is just taking the pop-up children's book concept into the digital age. (Alice from Atomic Antelope and Fox in Socks [Dr. Seuss], from Oceanhouse Media, are just two examples of apps for the iPad.)

On the negative side, apps that read stories aloud and require interaction change reading aloud from a social activity to an isolated pursuit. Isn't it a little like putting a child in front of a TV?

It's important to distinguish between books and games; for example, The Three Little Pigs, from Nosy Crow, is primarily a game.

Does a product that blurs the line between a book and a game destroy the joy of reading? One thing is for sure: a book is much more than an "iPad that doesn't work." Teachers and parents may use Kindles, laptops, iPads, and phones to read books, but they often say that they want their children surrounded by printed books.

The research on using electronic gadgets is thin. But you can be sure that it is important to have emerging readers experience actual paper pages as they learn about shapes, colors, and children's literature.

Teaching Tips for Emerging Readers and Writers

- Provide a print-rich language environment.
- Be sure that children can try out what they are learning about language.
- Encourage lots of interactive experiences in a risk-free environment.
- Reading and writing should be interrelated and should cut across subjects.
- Children should be given many choices about what they read and write.
- Meaning should be at the center of all language and literary experiences.
- Teachers should model reading and writing as authentic, fun, and dynamic processes.

Beginning readers may have to be repeatedly exposed to a book by hearing the story read well several times before they develop oral fluency themselves. The old-fashioned round-robin style doesn't work well. If you want to do a lot of oral reading, simply do paired reading in groups of two. Have the students get close to each other, point the chairs in opposite directions, and have them take turns reading. Don't assume that the student—or even an adult—can make a book sound exciting when reading out loud.

It takes a wide range of language and social skills for children to move smoothly through early literacy experiences. Some children don't know any letters when they enter school. Some know them all. There is no rush, but knowing a dozen or more letters upon entering kindergarten would be useful.

Early reading and prewriting skills include recognizing letters visually and aurally and understanding the role of letters in words and of words in giving meaning to stories. Making the jump to the printed word requires knowing that English is read from left to right. Students also have to know that the spaces between letters and punctuation are important.

While much of what students learn about math is learned at school, language and literacy have a lot to do with habits formed at home. A language-rich home environment has always been one of the keys to language learning. The message has gotten out to many parents that they should be reading to their children. But everyone seems less familiar with the importance of interactions during book reading, play sessions with toys, storytelling, and conversations during family meals.

Reading a book to a child can be much more than what's in the text—it may also involve having interesting conversations about the book. It is out of conversations about what is read and written that learners develop better oral language and reading skills. Also, the way students write is influenced by what they read and discuss.

Conversations expose children to new words, help them develop oral language skills, and build their pre-reading skills to the point where picking up a book comes naturally. Children's knowledge of spoken language supports reading, and reading experiences support language acquisition. Many aspects of early reading success can be traced to language-rich family environments.

Children learn some of their most important reading lessons at the dinner table. Mealtime is a young child's best opportunity to engage in interesting conversations with adults. As children learn to describe events, they also learn vocabulary and use newly acquired language skills to convey images and information. A home environment where parents and children read for fun is one of the keys to moving children in the direction of literacy.

Success in literacy activities in the early school years is critical because it is a strong predictor of overall academic success in the later grades. In moving up through the elementary grades, a major goal is to make reading and writing easier and more pleasurable (Chambliss and Valli, 2011).

Listening, singing, dancing, performing, and retelling what has been read and written and talking to others about the results certainly help the literacy process along. If everything goes according to plan, by the time children are in grade 5, they should be doing reasonably well in both reading and writing. As the middle school years progress, it is important for students to be prepared to read age-appropriate books in world literature, history, science, and other subjects.

The best way for learners to become good writers is by becoming good at understanding the complex sentence patterns and vivid diction found in good age-appropriate literature. In other words, reading well-written books helps generate good writing. A note of caution: the practice of continually breaking writing down into a narrow range of workbook-centered (fill-in-the-blank) skills cuts into the joyful and thoughtful expression of language.

IMAGINATIVE ACTIVITIES FOR EMERGING READERS AND WRITERS

Activity 1: Signs, Labels, Lists, and Charts

Teachers can display these items in the room and point to them when discussing what they label. Signs, labels, and their associates are functional, and children should be encouraged to use and read them. Examples: children's names on their desks, the teacher's name and room number on the door, calendar with dates/events, and poems/songs/chants.

Activity 2: Predictable Pattern Books

Some of these are based on familiar patterns, like the alphabet, numbers, days of the week, or seasons of the year. Other examples might be the familiar sequences in books like *Curious George* or *The Very Hungry Caterpillar*. Remember, good readers are good predictors.

Activity 3: Big Books and Shared Reading

Big books, with oversized pages and print, can be used to help children predict what will happen next. Many publishers have enlarged popular children's books. Teachers and students can create their own, or simply copy stories on paper large enough to be seen from fifteen feet away. If you want the books to last, think about laminating the big pictures and words created and inserting a metal ring or two at the top.

Young children can learn to appreciate good literature with the help of large print and colorful illustrations found in big books. Big books can also provide positive group reading experiences, while letting children observe the teacher engaged in an activity that they can emulate.

Reading Steps in Sharing a Big Book

- The teacher introduces the book and makes children predict what it is about.
- The teacher reads the book to the students and holds the book up high so the children can see the words.
- The teacher sometimes pauses so students can think about what will happen next.
- The teacher rereads the book, with students reading (out loud) along with him or her.

- Students may pair up for a rereading and take turns reading small parts.

Activity 4: Action Alphabet

This activity can help students identify letters and practice letter sounds. It can also help them use their bodies to form words, parts of words, and even sentences. Just ask them to stand up and make a letter with their body. Have the rest of the class guess the letter name and say the letter sound. You might also ask two students to work together to form one letter. You can move to two-, three-, or four-letter words. Rhyming or forming some of the parts of words is another possibility. Words might be taken from the books that the children are reading, or from a language experience story, or simply made up on the spot. The final step might be a sentence where each child becomes a letter; the last one in the line could become an exclamation point or a question mark.

Activity 5: Read, Talk, Draw, and Write

After the teacher reads the story aloud, he or she talks about it with the children and asks questions about the story and the artwork. Then students work in pairs or groups of three, using paper, crayons, felt pens, or paintbrushes to draw and write anything they want about the story that has been read. A storyboard (like a comic strip) or a three-, four-, or six-frame set of pictures with captions also works well.

Experienced teachers are well aware of the problems associated with old-style, round-robin reading. It slows down the good readers, embarrasses the poor readers, and results in students' simply saying words without comprehension. There are, however, some good ways to make meaning, with the ideas in a book, while reading aloud.

Activity 6: Writing a Story from Another Point of View

Take a story like *Jack and the Beanstalk* and tell it from the point of view of the giant. Bring it up to date and think about how you would feel if Jack had broken into your house. Suppose you were the giant. Do you want to get Jack jailed for burglary? Another example: write the *Three Little Pigs* from the point of view of the wolf. . . . Try for a little comedy (Wolf: "I was framed!").

Activity 7: A Sample Script Based on a Caldecott Award Winner

Children start with their backs to the audience. When it says "all" next to the story line, all the students in the group turn and read the line together. When it says "Voice #1" next to the story line, only the child assigned that line turns around (or stands up) and reads. For the numbers to work out right, you may have to ask some children to represent two "voices."

Drummer Hoff:

All: "Drummer Hoff fired it off."

Voice #1: "Private Parriage brought the carriage."

All: "But Drummer Hoff fired it off."

Voice #2: "Corporal Farrell brought the barrel.

Corporal Farrell brought the barrel."

Voice #1: "Private Parriage brought the carriage."

All: "But Drummer Hoff fired it off."

Voice #3: "Sergeant Chowder brought the powder."

All: "But Drummer Hoff fired it off."

Voice #2: "Corporal Farrell brought the barrel."

Voice #1: "Private Parriage brought the carriage."

All: "But Drummer Hoff fired it off."

Voice #4: "Captain Bammer brought the rammer.

Captain Bammer brought the rammer."

Voice #3: "Sargent Chowder brought the powder."

Voice #2: "Corporal Farrell brought the barrel."

Voice #1: "Private Parriage brought the carriage."

All: "But Drummer Hoff fired it off."

Voice #5: "Major Scott brought the shot."

Major Scott brought the shot."

Voice #4: "Captain Bammer brought the rammer."

Voice #3: "Sergeant Chowder brought the powder."

Voice #2: "Corporal Farrell brought the barrel."

Voice #1: "Private Parriage brought the carriage."

All: "But Drummer Hoff fired it off."

Voice #6: "General Border gave the order."

General Border gave the order."

Voice #5: "Major Scott brought the shot."

Voice #4: "Captain Bammer brought the rammer."

Voice #3: "Sergeant Chowder brought the powder."

Voice #2: "Corporal Farrell brought the barrel."

Voice #1: "Private Parriage brought the carriage."

All: "But Drummer Hoff fired it off."

Voice #6: "Ready . . . aim . . . FIRE!"

ALL: "KABAHBOOM!"

GROUP ACTIVITIES FOR ALL GRADES

Readers' theater: Small groups of four or five students can select a book that contains several characters who dialogue frequently. Passages may be rewritten to accommodate the readers' theater structure. Put four or five chairs in the front of the room so that students stand up when they read and sit down when not reading. Keep the lines fairly short and have one student read two roles if needed. One line might be repeated, as a refrain, after each character; on the refrain, everyone stands up and reads the line together. Students choose a character's lines to read, rehearse, and perform. The goal is to have the group present a narrative piece to the rest of the class, with solid intonation, inflection, and fluency.

Collaborative reading: Students are divided into pairs where they reread a story to each other. Another example might be taking turns reading the lines of a big book mounted on an easel.

Paired reading: Two or more students read aloud a passage that they have already read silently or that one student has read with the teacher.

Choral reading: This approach works with readers at any grade level. The teacher reads the story aloud to students, who follow along in their books. This is done as expressively as possible. Next, the students read a short passage (together) from the story in choral style, using the same intonation and punctuation signals as the teacher. In pairs or small groups, children can model the teacher and practice using their voices to express meanings (Butler, 2012).

Activity 6: Creative Drama

As in readers' theater, in creative drama there is no memorization of lines, and there is group support for the action. However, creative drama is different from readers' theater in many ways. The lines aren't written down and students usually do a short sixty- or eighty-second skit. You might, for example, ask a group of students to work together on an original ad. No props . . . or only a few. Quick action and humor go a long way.

1. Search the Internet for a copy of "The Dream Keeper" poem by Langston Hughes. Many websites have the copy of this poem including this website: http://allpoetry.com/poem/8495511-The_Dream_Keeper-by-Langston_Hughes
2. Have the groups discuss the poem and talk about their dreams.
3. Ask such questions as, "What is the best dream *you* ever had?"
4. Have them reread the poem in their own words.
5. Encourage them to write about their dreams in their journal: sleeping dreams, daydreams, thoughts about the future.

Activity for Creative Drama

Have students sit in small groups. Each one shares a dream. If someone can't remember a dream, have him or her use a daydream. Do a sixty-second skit on one of the dreams. When the group finishes, have the person who dreamed it explain it.

Poetry Structures for Sharing

Shape Poems

Words should be written to show the shape of the object being expressed. This is a fun exercise for any grade level.

> *"slippery . . .*
> *sliding . . .*
> *slithering . . . sensitive snake . . . "*

(Get the poem into the shape of whatever it is about.)

Syllable Poems

Writing syllable poems is challenging and also good practice for syllabication.

> *Now?*
> *Not me*
> *Not today*
> *The sun is bright*
> *Too hot for running*
> *I'd rather be*
> *inside, cool,*
> *and still*
> *Now!*

Couplets

Writing couplets is a good way to learn how to make rhymes. Also, couplets require more precise wordplay.

> *Ring the bell slowly*
> *The church is holy.*
> *Did you ever taste an ice cream*
> *Standing in a cold stream?*
> *Did you ever see a duck*
> *Hitting a hockey puck?*

When students have mastered writing simple rhyming couplets, let them try variations—for example, a couplet that does not rhyme but is a complete thought (a question and an answer or a description of an object.)

Cinquain

Start by providing a picture or artwork that shows some kind of action.

The first word: one word that is the subject of the picture.

The second words: two adjectives.

The third words: three verbs ending in -*ing*.

The fourth words: four words that say something about the picture.

The last word: one word to sum up.

> *Worry*
> *scary, tight*
> *writing, guessing, erasing*
> *hoping, fearing, risking, uncertain*
> *Test!*

Diamente

This is a poem that takes the shape of a diamond. It has seven contrasting lines. The first line is a noun; the second line has two adjectives describing the noun; and the third line has three *-ed* or *-ing* verb forms relating to the noun. The fourth line begins to make a transition by having four nouns that refer to both the opening and closing noun (line 7). (The noun in line 7 must have an opposite or contrasting meaning to the noun in line 1.) Line 5 has three *-ed* or *-ing* verb forms relating to the noun in line 7. Line 6 has two adjectives related to the last noun.

> *Desert*
> *sandy, windy*
> *basking, hardening, drying*
> *coyotes, cacti, rattlesnakes, yucca*
> *rising, cooling, changing*
> *fresh, crisp*
> *Mountains*

Japanese Lantern

This poetry form has five lines with eleven syllables in a one-two-three-four-one pattern.

One syllable _____
Two syllables _____
Three syllables _____
Four syllables _____
One syllable _____

Form Poems

Although form poems have a definite pattern, within the structure there is sufficient flexibility for all children to write something pleasing.

The stanza rhymes *a, b, a, b*. Each of the four lines is composed of types of words, such as nouns, verbs, adjectives, and adverbs. Every word is separated from the others by a comma. To think of the words, try association. Lines 1 and 3 contain four words; lines 2 and 4 contain three words.

_____ , _____ , _____ , _____
_____ , _____ , _____
_____ , _____ , _____ , _____
_____ , _____ , _____

> *Cloudy, dismal, dull, hazy,*
> *Gray, wet, dreary,*
> *Sleepy, dreamy, tired, lazy,*
> *Weak, hot, weary*

Found Poems

Have students create poems from words found in the environment around them. This is an effective way to focus the children's attention on something when the class is out on an excursion. Ask them to focus on signs, comments they hear, advertising slogans, or newspaper headlines. The found words can then be grouped to form a poem that becomes a poem on the excursion.

> *Stop & Look — special for today*
> *Oranges good for baby — good for you*
> *Buy a fresh pineapple — taste of tropical summer*
> *This has to be today's best buy!*
> *Fish tanks and all accessories*
> *Frog legs $5.50*
> *Why pay more?*

Summarize with Biopoems

Biopoems encourage students to make inferences, to synthesize, and to evaluate learning because the students must select precise language to fit the form and character. Biopoems are especially effective in literature and social science and are dynamic methods for students to introduce themselves to one another and the instructor. Instructors may also use the biopoem form to introduce themselves to the class.

Creating a Collaborative Biopoem

1. Divide the class into groups of two or three.
2. Each small group produces a biopoem about an author of a book, a historical figure, or someone from the newspaper. If it's an author, students will have to find some biographical information.
3. Give groups a large sheet of poster paper and some colorful markers. Instruct the groups to make a poster large enough for the class to see.
4. After the group has finished one biopoem, encourage individuals to do a biopoem about themselves.
5. At both stages, group members should be talking to one another and making comparisons.

The biopoem form is:

Line 1: first name _____
Line 2: four traits that describe the character _____
Line 3: relative (brother, sister, wife, husband, etc.) of _____
Line 4: lover of _____ (three things or people)
Line 5: who feels _____ (three items)
Line 6: who needs _____ (three items)

Line 7: who fears _____ (three items)
Line 8: who gives _____ (three items)
Line 9: who would like to see _____ (three items)
Line 10: resident of _____
Line 11: last name _____

Biopoem Uses

- To describe a character in a book
- To understand a historical or well-known figure
- To review insects, frogs, or animals
- To introduce people
- To develop a character before writing a story

COMMUNICATING AND THINKING STRATEGICALLY

Whether it's poetry, prose, or old or new media, the whole range of language skills can be helped by communicating with peers, who provide immediate feedback during the reading, writing, and revision process. Whatever the age of the students, the most competent readers tend to be the most competent talkers, listeners, writers, viewers, and thinkers. Successful programs immerse learners in reading and writing all day, with language lessons that are integrated throughout the curriculum.

The standards for the English language arts suggest that teachers help students learn to read and write strategically. This means constructing meaning by self-monitoring comprehension (questioning, reviewing, revising, and rereading). There is no one best way to teach reading, writing, or anything else. We can, however, point to directions that are supported by the research and explore some alternatives for getting around today's literacy-intensive world.

Many of the best ideas around today are remarkably simple. For example, if you want to teach reading or writing, then students should do a lot of it. And you can be sure that some student interaction and discussion will help the process along.

From informal suggestions to peer editing, there is a wide range of interactive group activities that can help with writing. When it comes to reading, children can also work in small groups to act out a story or practice reading the lines in a readers' theater activity. They can also work in small groups to discuss the theme, plot, characterization, or difficulty to be overcome in the story. (Felt pens and large paper can be used for semantic maps or webs of their answers.)

There are times when student work can be put up or printed and distributed so that the work is shared with the whole class. The most important thing is to get children thinking, discussing, and interacting with literature and with one another.

IMPORTANT POINTS FOR LEARNING

- The organization and arrangement of the physical environment
- An intellectual environment where ideas are valued and respect given
- A collaborative emotional-social environment that encourages risk taking
- Making sure that children are partly responsible for the quality of the class
- Promoting cooperation among children and building it into their daily activities
- Showing students how to assess their own learning and use of time

THE WRITING PROCESS

Writing . . . has three steps: thinking about it, doing it, and doing it again (and again and again, as often as time will allow and patience will endure). —Thomas S. Kane

The writing process is about how writers approach and perform writing. It involves planning, research, drafting, revising, editing, and sharing. Children come to school with a wide variety of experiences, vocabularies, social skills, and existing knowledge bases. For example, they begin writing or scribbling before they enter school. A child's writing develops through constant invention and reinvention of the forms of written language.

Since reading has a strong influence on writing, young writers need to *read* good writing. Story making and sharing are prime motivators for translating ideas into written text. As children interact with literate others and participate in literacy events, they become more adept at writing.

To develop their unique voice as writers, children must also be given plenty of time to write about their own ideas and concerns. Most writers find that good writing comes from revision. Feedback from their peers is a natural part of the process.

Working with others and writing every day may not guarantee the acquisition of skills like organizing, composing, elaborating, and revising, but it sure helps. So does having peers, parents, and teachers who know how to respond to a child's writing.

The development of a writing community is a very powerful way for students to collaborate in developing their writing voice. Along the way, young writers work together to draft, rethink ideas, research, revise, and edit. Writing processes are a set of mental procedures that comprise the act of writing. It is comprised of multiple elements that interact fluidly.

We suggest paying close attention to how children might approach and perform the writing task. Revision is the key to good writing. Rarely does a writer get it right the first time; usually the second draft is better. Although some writers can edit in their heads before putting something on paper, more commonly it takes a third or fourth time through to get the exact word, the apt phrase, the perfect metaphor.

The writing process is more recursive than linear. In other words, when writing takes place, students must return to their thinking, go back, rephrase, and think again (revise as they draft, or edit as they invent).

Good language and literacy instruction do not always follow a linear or stage-bound pattern. In fact, the research suggests that it doesn't make sense to strictly follow predetermined steps (Robinson, McKenna, and Conradi, 2011). Still, it may be useful to examine a writing process model that has had a major impact on instruction.

Teachers who have adopted this model help their students experience various dimensions of the writing process: prewriting, drafting, revising, editing, and publishing (sharing). *Prewriting* involves thinking about what might be written. Children can brainstorm ideas and outline stories or essays. For all the planning, writers are often surprised by what they write. We suggest expecting and hoping for the unexpected. Writing is a social process and ideas for composing and revising often come from our experiences with others. Group sharing helps students talk about their ideas with others before they write a first draft.

Drafting involves early attempts at getting ideas down on paper. As writers write (draft), they read and reread what they have written. Many teachers invite young authors to allow all their ideas to spill onto the page. Before students change (revise) what they have written, they make decisions about what to add, delete, or reorder so that they can do a better job of communicating with their audience.

Revising involves making changes in the draft. Writers tend to revise naturally—they erase and cross out information as they draft a story. Young students who are just learning how to form letters and write words should not be revising. Instead, they should be developing an interest in writing and looking at the purpose for writing. Authors can look at their own writing pieces to assess spelling, punctuation, or capitalization. Peers can give feedback through peer editing. Peer discussion and help with revision involve reasoning, comprehending, and reflecting. Students can become good at helping one another clarify what they want to say.

Editing is the next step. Writers usually correct (edit) their spelling, grammar, and punctuation after they feel that what they are writing has reached a stage where it might serve their purpose and that of their audience. Students revisit a piece of writing after they have revised and gone over it with a partner. Feedback like this helps students become more aware of how others react to their pieces.

Publishing or sharing with an audience is the final step in the writing process. Students can put their stories on the Internet, in the local newspaper, or in the school or classroom library. Some might read their stories out loud to a group of students in the classroom.

Jointly developed folders (portfolios) have a major role to play in student writing assessment. With selected samples, these folders can provide a running record of students' interests and what they can and can't do.

PEER WRITING GROUPS

To work toward less control, teachers need to help students take more responsibility for their own learning. The ability to evaluate does not come easily at first, and peer writing groups will need teacher-developed strategies to help them process what they have learned. The ability to reflect on being a member of a peer writing team is a form of "metacognition"—learning to think about thinking. The skills of productive group work may have to be made explicit. This requires processing in a circular or U-shaped group where all students can see one another.

Questions for evaluative social processing might include:

- How did group leadership evolve?
- Was it easy to get started?
- How did you feel if one of your ideas was left out?
- What did you do if most members of your group thought that you should write something differently?
- How did you rewrite?
- Did your paper say what you wanted it to?
- What kind of a setting do you like for writing?
- How can you arrange yourself in the classroom to make the writing process better?
- What writing tools did you use?
- How do you feel when you write?
- Explain the reasoning behind what you did.

(Remember, it's just as important for students to explain their reasoning as it is for them to express their feelings and preferences.)

For students at any level, the writing process can take the form of jointly produced language experience stories. These can be placed on large charts with the teacher or an upper grade student doing the writing.

CONNECTING READING AND WRITING WITH A LANGUAGE EXPERIENCE STORY

- Start with an experience that the children had.
- Talk about it in small groups.
- Write about it or have someone write it for you.
- If it can be written, then everyone can read it.

In the lower grades, language experience stories can be combined with pictures and made into a small or big book for the classroom library. If the children are too young to write, the teacher can write for them. Once children can write on their own, they can keep a private journal where they express their experiences and label their drawings and writing samples.

As students learn to expand their perspectives, they can begin to carry a story from one page (or day) to the next. Time may be set aside each day for a personal journal entry. Although it's important that the language be in a student's own words, the teacher can make comments without formal grading.

There are times when teachers have to intervene to assess students' writing or do some final editing before something is publicly shared. You might consider stamping "draft" or "creative writing—work in progress" on anything that might go home before it reaches its final form. A "work in progress" stamp would save everyone from a little embarrassment when a misspelled word or some bad grammar is seen by parents and school administrators.

MOVING UP THE ELEMENTARY GRADES WITH GRAPHIC ORGANIZERS

Graphic organizers are a useful strategy for developing and integrating knowledge. They can be used as a framework for writing or for improving comprehension after reading a story.

Story Planning Sheet

Directions. To write an imaginative story, you use the elements of narrative fiction: point of view, characters, setting, plot, high point, and outcome. At the top of the graphic organizer (below), write the point of view you have chosen to use. In the second space, write the main character or characters of your story. In the third space, describe the setting briefly. In the plot section of the organizer, first list the central conflict your main character faces, and then list the four main events of your story. The story should also have a high point and an outcome and these you list in the last two blocks of the organizer.

Graphic Organizer

Point of View

Characters

Setting

Plot/Main Character's Problem or Conflict

Event 1

Event 2

Event 3

Event 4

High Point

Outcome

STORY: _____

QUALITIES	*CHARACTERS*
Brave	
Cooperative	
Honest	
Polite	
Generous	
Confident	
Obedient	
Uncooperative	
Dishonest	
Rude	
Insecure	
Disobedient	

Compare Two Stories:

_____

Name _____

Write the setting, main characters, and the main problem of two stories.

	Story 1	*Story 2*
Title	_____	_____
Setting	_____	_____
Main Characters	_____	_____
Main Problem	_____	_____

SEMANTIC MAPS

Semantic maps are graphic representations that can help students understand the connections between concepts. The main concept goes in a large circle in the middle of the paper. Secondary ideas go out like spokes from the center of a wheel. Less-important ideas can come out on a line from spokes. Maps can be used for prediction or for summarizing what has been read. The size can range from a single page to a large sheet of paper that can be put up in the room.

STORYTELLING, DISCUSSION, READING, AND WRITING

Literature is one of the keys to literacy. To reach its full power, it must be integrated with the other language arts. Some of the connections occur naturally. For example, reading a well-written story can have a positive influence on writing. Another example is when students have a chance to talk to others about what they are reading.

With a little encouragement from the teacher, students can get better at listening to others for ideas, writing in their response journals, and dramatizing stories.

Connecting the story to creative drama and writing is a good way for students to share imaginative ideas with their peers. You might ask students to record how they think and make inferences about what they read. The whole process can create an atmosphere where unconscious thoughts can flow freely.

WRITING ORAL HISTORIES

Exploring the lives of elders in the community can be more than informative; it can make use of the full range of communication skills to connect generations. We like to invite five or six elders in for an oral history project. You might focus on a particular era by inviting individuals who lived through a certain era to explain the events of a particular time. Pictures and artifacts can help.

A good way to interview five or six elders (at the same time) is to put one in each small group where he or she can be interviewed by students who take notes and later write up the elder's "history." After a half hour or more, the teacher brings the whole class together and one student from each group introduces the elder from their group to the class and explains one or two subjects they covered.

The students need to do a little homework on the time period in question and prepare some questions. The local newspaper may even be willing to come in and cover the event. In a small town, the local newspaper might even carry the final version of what the students write about each visitor. Teachers and students often put some compositions and digitized photos on the Internet. It is also common to post some pictures and writing in the classroom or make it available in the library.

Physical books are declining in number relative to e-books. But book content lives on in a world where iPod Touches, iPads, Kindles, and Nooks come bundled with preloaded textbooks, books, and other curriculum materials. Still, in spite of all the gadgets, there is something very elegant about reading the printed word on paper.

Whatever combination of media teachers make use of, it sometimes makes sense to encourage students to use the Internet to share information with other students and with experts outside school. After all is said and done, disciplined and intelligent use of technology can encourage more learning outside school in a way that supports what's going on in the classroom.

As far as the Internet is concerned, using or setting up interactive Web sites can be useful; the same thing can said for small-group discussion. But it is even more important to make sure that students have significant periods set aside for actually reading books.

Even those who have questions about the Internet's significance are not necessarily indifferent to how expansive technological change can be.

Methods like reading out loud to students and sharing books and response projects all have a role in literacy learning. Students can also keep response journals and focus on a few favorite books through writing, art, drama, or a particular line of research.

Teachers usually set up response projects in a way that emphasizes reflection and interpretation rather than activities like summarizing the plot of a story. Along the way you can notice teacher and student interest in an author, illustrator, or theme. Students and teachers can even plan a unit together, choosing books around a topic or person of interest and planning reading and response activities.

ACTIVITIES

The kind of activities described here are built on a belief in collaborative learning and the complementary belief that reading and writing instruction should be natural, holistic, and connected to a strong literary base.

"Think-Aloud" Stories

Some teachers like to use what they call a "think-aloud." They choose one or two strategies to teach such as prediction, visualization, confirming, elaborating, or summarizing. Next, they talk about how they use these strategies to activate prior knowledge as they read. The next step is to have the students practice the meaning-construction strategy—working with a partner as they read, thinking out loud, and jotting down a few notes. This helps students develop their own critical reading and writing skills as they experience a variety of viewpoints.

Reader Response

Putting the reader response theory into practice involves arranging the classroom for group discussions. Literature circles, creative writing, and dramatic activities are all part of the process. The basic idea is to actively engage students in what they are reading by encouraging them to express their feelings and understandings. The next step might be to have students talk to one another about the connection between literature and actual situations that they know from experience or real people about whom they have read (Bower, 2011).

Bookmark Response and Sharing

The teacher prepares bookmarks to suggest how children might respond to the story they are reading. For example: What song does this book remind you of? What character would you like to interview (and why)? If you were to paint a scene from this story, what part would you choose?

Sustained Silent Reading (SSR)

This approach can form a major part of any reading program. It involves reading every day by everyone in the classroom, including the teacher. SSR is designed to build positive attitudes toward reading. Children pick their own books. The time period frequently ranges from five to fifteen minutes. Teachers often put a "do not disturb" sign on the classroom door so that reading is viewed as more important than disruptions from the outside.

You may want to post the rules:

- Everyone in the room reads during SSR.
- There will be no interruptions or talking.
- You will not be asked to report on what you have read.
- SSR time will be for ____ minutes, every day starting at ____ and ending at _____ .

(This simple chart will provide a helpful reminder for the children.)

Competence in all subject areas is dependent on competency in reading, writing, and the other language arts. As in other basic disciplines, standards for language arts classroom instruction should be based on the best research and most current knowledge about subject matter. The language arts standards offer a set of research-based guidelines defining what students should know and be able to do in the language arts. None of the standards are carved in stone, but they do represent a comprehensible document that can be used to support instruction, ensure quality assessment, and provide guidance for the future.

OVERVIEW OF THE STANDARDS FOR THE ENGLISH LANGUAGE ARTS

All students should:

- Read a wide range of print and nonprint texts to build an understanding of texts, of themselves, and of other cultures
- Read a broad selection of literature from many periods, in many genres to acquire an understanding of the many dimensions of the human experience
- Apply many strategies to comprehend, interpret, evaluate, and appreciate texts
- Adjust their use of spoken, written, and visual language to communicate effectively with a wide variety of audiences
- Use a wide array of writing strategies to communicate with different audiences for a variety of purposes
- Apply knowledge of language structure (including spelling and punctuation) to ensure their writing is well received and understood
- Use spoken, written, and visual language to accomplish their own purposes (National Council of Teachers of English and International Reading Association, 1996).

LANGUAGE, LITERACY, AND CREATIVITY AS SHARED EXPERIENCES

By giving students regular opportunities to talk, read, write, go online, and solve problems together, language learning really comes alive. Teamwork skills help students maintain a healthy balance between believing that they have the ability to learn and knowing that their efforts will help them maximize their ability.

From online library books to search inquiries and Wikipedia entries, it is now possible to identify certain patterns of human behavior. For example, social scientists, cognitive psychologists, and computer specialists are beginning to tap vast data resources and develop predictive algorithms that can help them make tentative predictions about certain aspects of learning and the future in general (Malone, Laubacher, and Dellarocas, 2010).

Active team learning provides students with opportunities to jointly interpret and negotiate meaning as they work together to make connections between prior knowledge and new ideas. Collaboration and preparation are two of the keys to opening up new ideas; it is rare for innovation to just come out of the blue.

Language learning is, at its best, a shared creative experience. At home, this means stories at bedtime, discussions about the news, having adults who read, museum excursions, and library visits. At school, it means encouraging a cooperative environment so that students can actively construct knowledge together and perform alone when they need to. To paraphrase Vygotsky, what children can do together today, they can do and love tomorrow.

When it comes to creativity and innovation, *execution* is just as important as generating new ideas. After all, someone has to figure out how to pull the diverse strands of insights together in a practical way and spread the word or invention.

Helping an innovation to reach its promise requires a blend of creativity and discipline. Those who can bring something new to life tend to have a more disciplined and empirical side that can cut through chaotic and uncertain situations. Also, successful innovators often have the ability to get a higher return on luck when it is staring them in the face (Collins and Hansen, 2011).

The changes in technology and instruction are colliding in today's classrooms. Our whiz-bang digital gadgets may—or may not—add much to academic achievement. But they can encourage creative thinking and innovation by amplifying idea exchange and healthy debate. You can also be sure that coming to educational terms with technology will be part of any serious discussion about curriculum and instruction in tomorrow's schools.

LITERACY IN A DIGITAL AGE

No matter what approach you take to reading and writing instruction, it is important to pay close attention to background knowledge, reader-writer transactions, and social interaction. Imaginative writing activities and good literature for children and young adults also matter. There is even some evidence that literature-based experiences and creative writing can encourage independent thinking, imaginative problem solving, and teamwork (Street and Lefstein, 2007).

Being able to work with and evaluate all the media-related possibilities that now surround us are now part of any essential skills package. As technology sales pitches become ever more sophisticated, there is surprisingly little impartial evidence that high-tech products actually improve student achievement.

Any powerful approach to literacy development requires intrinsically motivating activities and helping children draw on their cultural and personal resources. Teachers need a fundamental knowledge of what they are teaching. But they also need to be able to understand how children learn and the different points of view that they bring to learning. At any level of schooling, understanding the environment that students are in is important as you go about helping learners develop productive habits of the mind.

A common element in successful schools (and classrooms) is a shared sense of community and a socially integrating sense of purpose. Starting with the child's own experiences and background knowledge, the collaborative process can lead to both a shared group idea and more elegant individual expression. Small collaborative groups need time to share, clarify, suggest, and expand concepts.

Reading and writing programs with connected spoken language and literature components provide a solid foundation for approaching instruction naturally and interactively.

Engaging youngsters in an active group exploration of ideas is an exciting and powerful way for children to take a dynamic role in their learning community. This supports the current standards in language arts that suggest helping students learn a wide range of strategies so that they can comprehend, evaluate, and appreciate spoken, written, and visual language.

Research and accountability are two of the keys needed to develop better methods of teaching reading and writing. But it is important to remember the old adage that not everything that can be counted counts, and not everything that counts can be counted.

To paraphrase T. S. Elliot, there is a shadow between conception, creation, and implementation (Isaacson, 2011). In other words, there are gaps separating conception, creation, and implementation. At its best, innovation involves moving from what we know should be done to making positive things actually happen. Having some idea about how change is happening in the twenty-first century is becoming part of what an influential teacher needs to know.

CONCLUSION AND LOOKING AHEAD

Certain simple truths about learning are sometimes lost in the smoky quarrelsomeness of the American education debate. One of these truths is that language and literacy learning are social. Also, instruction is most effective when it is holistic and placed within an authentic context.

When it comes to specific lessons, it is best to arrange things so that students can learn to read, write, talk, listen, reason, solve problems, and work together for real purposes that are important to them.

There is more at stake in language and literacy learning than academic achievement. Literacy in the twenty-first century includes being able to go beyond comprehension and production to understand how the information we receive and use is shaped. Such context-sensitive reading is necessary for meaningful civic engagement, social action, and democracy itself (Shannon, 2011).

There is increasing attention to critical thinking, insights, teamwork, and how literacy influences society. Still, as the twenty-first century progresses, literacy instruction will continue to focus on the core skills of reading and writing. As learners share knowledge with their peers, the seeds of literacy and imagination can grow, allowing students to adjust what they are doing and using in a way that speaks effectively to a variety of audiences.

By learning to use the communication tools associated with reading, writing, and the other language arts, learners can move on to appreciate, integrate, and apply what they learn at school, at home, and in the community. Literacy goes a long way toward preparing individuals who can build the world of tomorrow (Winch et al., 2011).

The future gets constructed in fits and starts as groups and individuals dream, tinker, build, test, and learn from their failures. Sitting back and trying to accurately predict what is going to happen in the coming years is futile. But there is at least some truth in the notion that the best way to predict the future is to be involved in making it.

Good preparation and exploring the possibilities put you in a better position to contribute to the construction of brave new worlds.

In spite of the limitations of educational technology, it is important to prepare students in a way that helps them thrive in an increasingly digital world. With the help of a rich school environment, youngsters can better approach, understand, and deal with what Shakespeare called "the brightest heaven of invention."

The specific methods with which a teacher chooses to teach reading and writing reflect a unique combination of professional knowledge, policy requirements, personal choice, and passion for the subject being taught.

Like successful innovators, good teachers take surprisingly different paths. Common factors in making a positive difference are tenacity, belief, and the patience to stay the course. Whether it's technological or educational change, informed enthusiasm is a common trait that leads to success.

For the seeds of literacy and the imagination to grow, teachers must act as energetic agents of change who arrange the classroom for cooperation and academic engagement. When teachers are truly energized, their students are more likely to communicate with others and make sense of the world around them. As William Blake has suggested, energy is an external delight.

SUGGESTED RESOURCES

Blake, W., and D. Erdman (Eds.). (1988). *The complete poetry and prose of William Blake.* New York: Anchor Books (Random House).

Burgin, R. (1968). *Conversation with Jorge Luis Borges.* Austin, TX: Holt, Rinehart, & Winston.

Google Art Project: www.googleartproject.com. This online art collection has works in dozens of media and materials from over 150 museums and arts organizations worldwide.

Murray, J. (1997). *Hamlet on the holodeck: The future of narrative in cyberspace.* New York: Free Press.

Powers, W. (2011). *Hamlet's BlackBerry: Building a good life in the digital age.* New York: Harper Perennial.

Vygotsky, L. S. (1978). *Mind in society: The development of higher educational processes.* Cambridge, MA: Harvard University Press.

Whitehead, A. N. (1929). *The aims of education.* New York: Macmillan.

REFERENCES

Austin, R., L. Devin, and E. Sullivan. (2011). Accidental innovation: Supporting valuable unpredictability in the creative process. *Organization Science* (forthcoming).

Bower, V. (Ed.). (2011). *Creative ways to teach literacy: Ideas for children aged 3 to 11.* Thousand Oaks, CA: Sage.

Boyd, M., and L. Galda. (2011). *Real talk in elementary classrooms: Effective oral language practice.* New York: Guilford.

Butler, H. (2012). *Classroom literacy games: Fun-packed activities for ages 7–13.* New York: Routledge.

Carter, J. (2007). *Building literacy connections with graphic novels: Page by page, panel by panel.* Urbana, IL: National Council of Teachers of English.

Chambliss, M., and L. Valli. (2011). *Upper elementary reading lessons: Case studies of real teaching.* Lanham, MD: Rowman & Littlefield.

Collins, J., and M. Hansen. (2011). *Great by choice: Uncertainty, chaos, and luck—why some thrive despite them all*. New York: HarperCollins.

Hall, L., L. Burns, and E. Edwards. (2011). *Empowering struggling readers: Practices for the middle grades*. New York: Guilford.

Isaacson, W. (2011). *Steve Jobs*. New York: Simon & Schuster.

Kane, T. (1994). *The new Oxford guide to writing*. Oxford: Oxford University Press.

Malone, T. W., R. Laubacher, and C. Dellarocas. (2010). The collective intelligence genome. *Sloan Management Review* 5, no. 3 (Spring): 21–31.

National Council of Teachers of English and International Reading Association. (1996). *Standards for the English language arts*. Urbana, IL, and Newark, DE: NCTE and IRA.

Randall, L. (2011). *Knocking on heaven's door: How physics and scientific thinking illuminate the universe and the modern world*. New York: HarperCollins.

Robinson, D., M. McKenna, and K. Conradi. (2011). *Issues and trends in literacy education*. 5th ed. Boston: Allyn & Bacon.

Schmidt, P., and A. Lazar (Eds.). (2011). *Practicing what we teach: How culturally responsive classrooms make a difference*. New York: Teachers College Press.

Shannon, P. (2011). *Reading wide awake: Politics, pedagogies, and possibilities*. New York: Teachers College Press.

Street, B., and A. Lefstein. (2007). *Literacy: An advanced resource book*. New York: Routledge.

Welner, K. G., P. H. Hinchey, and A. Molnar. (2010). *Think tank research quality: Lessons for policy makers, the media, and the public*. Scottsdale, AZ: Information Age Publishing.

Winch, G., R. R. Johnston, P. March, L. Ljungdahl, and M. Holliday. (2011). *Literacy: Reading, writing, and children's literature*. Oxford: Oxford University Press.

SEVEN

Arts Education

Connections, Knowledge, and Informed Encounters

> Building upon existing ideas and inventions is another way to foster innovation. In fact, when you ask artists of all types where they get their inspiration, they can usually list others before them who set the stage for their work. —T. Seeling

Many twenty-first-century models of education suggest that the arts can serve as a connection within and across disciplines. Projects involving the arts can also serve as a prism that allows students to connect with multiple subjects, dimensions, and directions of focus (Gardner, 2011).

As teachers try to plug critical thinking and cooperative learning into subject matter, the arts can help with synthesis, interconnection, and generating a sense of community.

In the arts, as in other subjects, no part of a composition is independent of the whole in which it participates. Whether it is the visual arts, music, dance, or drama, the arts have the possibility of providing active entry points to critical thinking, collaboration, and global skills. The challenge is building on that potential in ways that make educational possibilities a reality.

Arts education still pays close attention to actually *doing* art. But as the twenty-first century progresses, art instructors are paying more attention to culture, aesthetics, technology, and how the arts relate to other subjects.

Most school districts require some form of arts education, but the quality and emphasis vary greatly. National content standards in arts education are playing an important role in quality control—as well as supporting the effort to develop assessment techniques to measure student achievement in the arts.

155

New media can sometimes be a powerful amplifier for arts education. A good example is how images of visual art from museums around the world can be studied and analyzed online. Digital technology can also influence music education by making sampling and blending music relatively easy by providing students with the digital tools needed to mix and edit the compositions of others as they add pieces of their own composition.

Teaching students how the arts interconnect with one another and across the curriculum is a step toward powerfully engaging learners in all subjects.

The visual arts, dance, poetry, plays, and music have long been organizers or points of integration for a whole range of human activities. The merger of globalization and information technology requires that we all adapt more quickly, work smarter, and better understand the world. Along with helping students deal with a connected world the arts can enhance awareness of the aesthetic qualities of their own surroundings (Zwiers and Crawford, 2011).

The arts have a lot to do with enshrining some reproduction of experience, gaining some control over the process, and influencing the future. Encounters with the arts also have a unique capacity to provide openings for imaginative breaks from the expected. They continue the universal human practice of making special certain objects, sounds, movement, or representations that have been linked with human survival for countless generations.

PROVIDING A SENSE OF OPENING

Real artists pick up hints of cultural and technological challenges well before they result in transforming changes. Using new media to create art is but one example that students could study and emulate. David Hockney, for example, likes to turn digital play with his iPhone and iPad into on-screen images and paintings. He has even called the iPad the "most spontaneous medium" he has ever found.

The *Globe and Mail* newspaper (July 26, 2011) reports that David Hockney likes using his digital gadgets for "luminous subjects like landscapes, plants, sunrises and sunsets." This highly regarded artist has exhibited his digital artwork in museums. He also likes spontaneously drawing informal "iPictures" and sending them to friends.

Hockney has a history of constructing artwork with a wide range of media for a variety of purposes. He has made use of paint, photography, computers, fax machines, photocopiers, and opera set design. In every case the medium has always influenced—and often determined—the end result.

You can use some of Hockney's approaches in the classroom.

With the help of two elementary school teachers we tried one of his techniques with fifth- and sixth-grade students. He calls the method we used a "joiner."

Our approach: Students were put into teams of two or three and asked to take pictures of the same thing from different distances and slightly different angles. For example, students used cameras to take seven or eight pictures of each other and/or things in the environment. The next day the teacher brought in the prints, students made an arrangement, and glued or taped them on construction paper. (Some of the students liked laminating the end result.) Finally, the results were posted in the room and in the hallway.

A sixth-grade teacher had her student teams use a digital camera to compose a "joiner" and printed the pictures (immediately) right in the room. The same art construction procedure was followed, but the lesson went from start to finish in one class period. (Note: some students started by going online to see how Hockney did it.)

The arts have always provided a space, a sense of opening, a loving of the question, and a unique communal resource. Today's school reform process should not push aside such a basic aspect of social consciousness and interdisciplinary knowing. If there are no arts in a school, there are fewer alternatives to exploring subjects by the spoken and written word.

The arts can open some collective doors of the mind and provide new spaces for the active construction of knowledge. Also, they are a powerful tool for countering the tendency toward standardization. Of course, at the classroom level it will take the skill of teachers to move forward and use the arts to shape the interconnected exuberance of learning—keeping light from the arts at the center of the human spirit.

Extending education in the arts with other subjects must go hand in hand with other new aspects of schooling and daily life. The notion that the arts can encourage wonder, inquiry, speculation, and technological literacy has for too long been lost in a morass of indifference, nostalgia, crafts, didacticism, and an already overcrowded curriculum. To dig it out requires a greater emphasis on professional development to help teachers become more familiar with the arts and discipline-based arts education.

There is an increasing trend for teachers around the world to be asked to encourage students across a number of art forms. These art forms include painting, photography, music, drama, media, technology, dance, and performance (Sinclair, Jeanneret, and O'Toole, 2008).

Whatever waves of change sweep over the schools, performance, creation, and understanding will continue to be important. However, arts education is becoming a little more focused on analysis, history, and culture. In the field this is referred to as a "discipline-based approach." It depends more than ever on the intellectual preparation and commitment of the teacher. Specialists can help, but it is the regular classroom teacher who will continue to be the primary source for instruction in the arts.

BRINGING THE ARTS TO THE PEOPLE

Even at the beginning of human civilization, the arts had a central place in ceremonies that connected cave paintings to ritual, religion, and daily life. Some predict that in the future our culture will be as filled with the arts as it now is with television and sports. Of course, a lot depends on how far you stretch the definition.

From the arts to the sciences, those involved are always looking for interesting problems to solve. Making or exploring something that we are unfamiliar with is the essence of creativity across subjects. And we all have a certain amount of creativity in us. Artists need feedback from others, and there is always a collective influence; it isn't working alone to create a masterpiece.

The arts are viewed by some as central to the twenty-first-century curriculum (Eisner, 2005). Many educators and artists argue that children without knowledge of the arts are as ignorant as children without knowledge of literature or math.

De Tocqueville predicted that American democracy would diminish the character of art. It took decades to prove him wrong—at least for a while. Now some artists have worked hard to break down the disconnection between the nation's establishment (including the arts, academia, and the press) and the people.

Whether it's visual arts, music, or the theater, the arts have the potential to help us be receptive to new thinking and generous toward the production of something fresh. Far from being beaten down, American artistic expressions, especially film and music, have been some of our most successful exports.

Some people think of the arts as elitist, therapeutic, frivolous, impractical, or mindless entertainment. They are not always wrong, but they miss the point. The arts can provide important intellectual tools for understanding many subjects. They also build on qualities that are essential to revitalizing schooling: teamwork, analytical thinking, motivation, and self-discipline.

In the twenty-first century, the arts have a lot to offer new approaches to curriculum and instruction. For example, skills and perspectives of art show what thinking, learning, and life can be. The arts also provide cultural resources that people can draw on for the rest of their lives (Donahue and Stuart, 2010). But in this era of accountability, attention has to be given to the substance of the disciplines involved. Otherwise the arts may be dismissed as expendable in an era of curriculum gridlock and financial difficulties.

VISUAL ANALYSIS AND THE CRITICAL FUNCTION OF THE ARTS

Efforts are now being made to deepen and extend education in the arts by connecting them to critical thinking, problem solving, aesthetic analysis, technology, and new ways of working. This increasing influence of discipline-based art education (DBAE) curriculum addresses more than the traditional issues of creative expression and performance. It provides an interdisciplinary framework for connecting arts education to aesthetic criticism within a cultural, historical, and social context.

In a literature-based reading curriculum, for example, students are expected to develop the thinking skills necessary for "literary criticism." Should we expect less when it comes to the arts? A renewed emphasis on artists, criticism, aesthetic discourse, and the importance of discipline-based arts education will accompany education into the next century.

Some Examples of Discipline-Based Art Education Activities: Practical Ideas for Teachers

The following discipline-based art activities are organized around an interdisciplinary unit theme entitled "You and Your World." This approach was selected so that critical thinking skills and interdisciplinary content could be linked and included as an integral part of classroom life.

As part of an integrated approach, it is important that children learn to be more flexible and to move freely between different communications media. To accomplish this, children need exposure to many different communication forms.

Unit Introduction Activity

Before beginning this unit, discuss with children the need all people have to communicate ideas and how there are many ways to this. Encourage children to brainstorm all the ways people use to communicate. List the suggestions on the board or on a chart. Young children may wish to find or draw pictures that can be placed on a bulletin board. Such a chart becomes an ongoing resource for students to refer to, and additions can be incorporated throughout the year.

Unit: You and the World

When you think of how you are related to others, the thing that most people say is family. But even if you were alone in the world, you wouldn't be unrelated. The fact that you have read these words makes you a member of the group of English-speaking people. As a student you have a relationship with those who attend your school and with those who work there. The music you listen to and enjoy is enjoyed by others. Your relationships with your fellow humans are marked by the foods you think are good, the clothes you think are fashionable, the jokes you tell.

In the nineteenth century, Ralph Waldo Emerson viewed the relationship between the arts and your day-to-day work with others as central to imaginative thinking. He felt that people depended on their relationships in order to understand what they read, wrote, painted, or sang. Emerson thought that each person is related to a few others and to all people; each of us has within ourselves the sum of human history.

You may never have thought of yourself as part of an ongoing historical record. But chances are you have watched characters in movies or on television and sensed that they felt as you have felt and acted as you would have acted, that they were, in a sense, related to you. Your relationships with actual or fictional others are the basis of sympathy and one of the keys to imaginative thinking.

Unit Activities

1. Make a map of significant relationships in your life. Put your name in the center of a sheet of paper. Then begin thinking of the important people in your life. As you think of them, write their names on the paper. Organize or group the names that belong together. You may wish to connect the names with lines to show the relationships.
2. Make a list of ten words you chose at random from the dictionary. Next write or make up something about yourself that uses all the words you have listed. It could be a paragraph in the form of a news report, a story, a creative drama—whatever works with the words you have. Just make sure you *use* the words, not just mention them.

   > For example, take the word *hare.*
   > Use: I saw a <u>hare</u>, chewing on a carrot in my garden.
   > Mention: <u>Hare</u> is another word for a rabbit.
   > Let the words guide what you write.

3. Suppose there is a lottery in your state. A three-digit number is picked at random. For $1 you can buy a ticket picking any number from 000 to 999. If the number on your ticket matches the number on the ticket drawn, you win $500. Is that a good payoff? Why or why not? How much of the money the state takes in does it keep?
4. Try reflecting on and then describing an episode from a television series that you regularly watch. Here are some questions that may help you think about the program. Jot down your answers. Then write a paragraph or two about what you've learned.

   a. For what sorts of people is the program produced?

b. Are the main characters people like you? Are they people you want to be like?

c. Are the main characters unusual in some way? If so, in what way? Are they usually attractive? Do they have special skills?

d. If the program is a comedy, what are the jokes about? Is there a laugh track? Do you laugh as often as you hear people in the audience laughing?

e. What kinds of problems do the characters in the program have? Are they the same sorts of problems you have?

f. Are the characters in the program richer or poorer than you are?

g. Describe the plot. Does it make sense? Do the characters in the program act the way real people act?

h. Does the program use background music? What sort of music? What does the music contribute to the mood of the program?

i. Try looking at the program without listening to the sound. What do you notice? Try listening to the program without watching the picture. What do you notice?

j. Do you know what is going to happen before it happens or are you surprised? How do you feel when the program ends?

CONNECTING SUBJECT MATTER WITH THE ARTS

The arts can also help get a dialogue going between disciplines that often ignore each other. When knowledge from diverse subject matter areas is brought together, the result can be a new and valuable way of looking at the world. The arts and humanities have proved very useful tools for integrating curricular areas and helping students transcend narrow subject matter concerns.

Teachers at many levels have used intellectual tools from the fine arts as a thematic lens for examining diverse subjects. Some schools have even worked out an integrated school day, where interdisciplinary themes based on the fine arts add interest, meaning, and function to collaboration. Whether it's reading, writing, arithmetic, or anything else, the arts can be wrapped around central themes in the arts so that rich connections stimulate the mind and the senses.

The research suggests that using a thematic approach improves students' knowledge of subject matter and aids in the transfer of the skills learned to other domains outside school. An additional finding is that good units organized around themes can improve the students' abilities to apply their knowledge to new subjects. In art, for example, language development flourishes when children are encouraged to discuss the materials they are using and reflect on the nature of their artwork through writing. Whatever the combination, an important result of integrating various subjects around a theme results in an enhancement of thinking and learning skills—the *metacurriculum*.

Before we can deal with teaching the thinking process, children need some solid content to think about. After that, teachers need to provide continuity between activities and subjects. The thinking skills engendered in one area can serve as a connection between subjects. In making curriculum connections, it's often helpful for teachers to see model lessons that include cross-disciplinary suggestions and activities.

The relationships established between subjects and the way teachers facilitate these relationships are important. When disciplines are integrated around a central concept, students can practice the skills that they have learned from many subjects. This helps students make sense out of the world.

The goal of an interdisciplinary curriculum is to bring together different perspectives so that diverse intellectual tools can be applied to a common theme, issue, or problem. Thematic approaches can help by providing a group experience that fosters thinking and learning skills that will serve students in the larger world. By its very definition, "interdisciplinary" implies cooperation among disciplines and people. The notion that students of different abilities and backgrounds can learn from one another is a natural outgrowth of the collaborative tendency inherent in this approach. Everyone's collaborative involvement not only allows input into the planning process, but can help with self-responsibility and long-term commitment to learning.

Organizing parts of the curriculum around themes means that each subject is mutually reinforcing and connected to lifelong learning. Subjects from the Greek classics to radiation theory need the historical, philosophical and aesthetic perspective afforded by interdisciplinary connections. Curriculum integration provides active linkages between areas of knowledge and consciously applies language and methods from more than one discipline to examine a central theme, issue, topic, or experience. This holistic approach focuses on themes and problems and deals with them more in depth rather than through memorizing facts and covering the text from cover to cover.

There is always the danger of watering down content in an attempt to cover all areas. We can, however, teach the work of Newton on one hand while paying attention to the history of the times on the other. The history of ideas, political movements, and changing relationships among people are part of the fabric of our world. We cannot narrowly train people in specialist areas and expect them to be able to deal with the multifaceted nature of twenty-first-century jobs.

THEMATIC STRATEGIES FOR CONNECTING SUBJECTS AND PEOPLE

Like the arts, innovation in science can experience ups and downs and culs-de-sac. These different ways of knowing, the arts and the sciences, do not need to grow farther apart. The unity of all cultural and scientific efforts was the unwritten rule until the eighteenth century. But as art and science have progressed over the last two hundred years, both have become more narrow, specialized, and extensive.

Whether the collaboration is in the distant past, a computer chip, or a peer sitting nearby, collaboration in art involves creating, interpreting, and connecting to others. Socially useful art requires hard thinking about the location and the intended audience in order to understand how best to engage local modes of expression and needs.

Themes can also direct the design of classroom activities by connecting classroom activities and providing them with a logical sequence and scope of instruction.

One set of steps for developing thematic concepts is to:

1. Determine what students know about a topic before beginning instruction. This is done by careful questioning and discussion.
2. Be sensitive to and capitalize on students' knowledge.
3. Use a variety of instructional techniques to help students achieve conceptual understanding.
4. Include all students in discussions and cooperative learning situations.

Thematic instruction values depth over breadth of coverage. The content should be chosen on how well it represents what is currently known in the field and its potential for dynamically making connections.

THEMATIC UNITS

The design of thematic units brings together a full range of disciplines in the school's curriculum: language arts, science, social studies, math, art, physical education, and music. Using a broad range of discipline-based perspectives can result in units that last an hour, a day, a few weeks, or a semester. They are not intended to replace a discipline-based approach, but they act as supportive structures that foster the comprehensive study of a topic.

Teachers can plan their interdisciplinary work around issues and themes that emerge from their ongoing curriculum. Deliberate steps can be taken to create a meaningful and carefully orchestrated program that is more stimulating and motivating for students and teachers. Of course, shorter flexible units of study are easier to do than setting up a semester or yearlong thematic unit.

Collaborative thematic curriculum models require a change in how teachers go about their work. It takes planning and energy to create effective integrated lessons, and more time is often needed for subject matter research because teachers frequently find themselves exploring and teaching new material. Thematic teaching also means planning lessons that use untraditional approaches, arranging for field trips, guest speakers, and special events.

Contacting parents, staff members, and community resources who can help expand the learning environment is another factor in the teacher's time and planning efforts. Long-range planning and professional development for teachers are other important elements of the process.

The arts have a power beyond aesthetics or making us "see." They can also enhance the ability (flexibility) to change your mind in the light of new information (McGrayne, 2011).

The arts can help us view ourselves, the environment, and the future differently—even challenging our certainties about the arts themselves. In connecting the basic concerns of history, civilization, thought, and culture, the arts provide spatial, kinesthetic, and aesthetic skills that are the foundation to what it means to be an educated person. Such understandings do not occur spontaneously. They have to be taught.

The process of understanding or creating in the arts is more than unguided play, self-expression, or a tonic for contentment. The arts can be tools for shattering stereotypes, changing behavior, building a sense of community, and a vehicle for sociopolitical commentary. An example from the visual arts: Barbara Kruger develops popular imagery that merges words and concepts from other disciplines. Along with other postmodernist artists (like Keith Haring and Jenny Holtzman), she works outside the artistic and the aesthetic frame to harness the formative power of images to affect deep structures of personal and social belief.

In a similar manner, artist Alexis Smith combines quotes, flotsam, and jetsam that speak to the artifices and pitfalls of a mythical America. When the right object is connected to the perfect quote, the result can range from the humorous to the toughest and most intriguing social observation. Moving toward music, storytelling, and dance, Lori Anderson extends the edges with performance art, combining nearly every basic art form with literary references and video imagery to create theatrical performances. Like many modern artists, she releases possibilities by making use of collaborators across time, media, and subject matter.

OPENING UP A SHARED SENSE OF WONDER

There is a connection between productive citizenship, academics, and the arts. For students to make these connections, it will take more than a specialist in the art class for one hour a week or an inspirational theater troupe visiting the school once a year. These brief experiences can help and inspire—but it takes more sustained work in the arts to make a real difference.

Quick "drive-by teaching" is the equivalent of driving a motorcycle through an art gallery: you might get some blurred notion of color but not much else. Cutting out daily arts education denies students a vital quality-of-life experience—expression, discovery, and an understanding of the chances for human achievement (Donahue and Stuart, 2010).

The arts can open up a sense of wonder and provide students with intellectual tools for engaging in a shared search. This won't occur if children are having fewer experiences with the arts at school and in their daily lives. They at least have to know enough to recognize what to notice and what to ignore. This means that some grasp of the discipline is required if the arts are going to awaken anyone to the possibilities of thoughtfulness, collaboration, and life.

There are some excellent models or prototypes of art education. The Minneapolis discipline-based art program is one example. Another is in Augusta, Georgia, where the National Endowment for the Arts (NEA) has supported the development of an exemplary arts education model. This program uses the arts to improve academic achievement, the general learning environment, student self-esteem, attendance, creative thinking, and social equity among students.

ART ACTIVITIES THAT ENCOURAGE REFLECTION

Reflecting is a special kind of thinking. Reflective thinking is both active and controlled. When ideas pass aimlessly through a person's mind, or someone tells a story that triggers a memory, that is not reflecting. Reflecting means focusing attention. It means weighing, considering, choosing. Suppose you want to drive home: you get the key out of your pocket, unlock the car door, and open the door. Getting into your car does not require reflection. But suppose you reached into your pocket and couldn't find the key. To get into your car requires reflection. You have to think about what you are going to do. You have to consider possibilities and imagine alternatives.

A carefully balanced combination of direct instruction, self-monitoring, and reflective thinking helps meet diverse student needs. The activities suggested here are designed to encourage higher-order thinking and learning and provide a collaborative vehicle for arts education.

Activity 1: Looking at the Familiar, Differently

Students are asked to empty their purses and pockets onto a white sheet of paper and create a face using as few of the items as possible. For example, one face might be simply a pair of sunglasses, another a single earring representing a mouth, and a third could be a profile created by a necklace forming a forehead, nose, and chin. This activity gives students a different way of looking at things. It's also an example of a teaching concept known as *aesthetic education.*

Activity 2: Collage Photo Art

Students at all levels can become producers as well as consumers of art. We used a videotape of David Hockney's work from *Art in America.* Hockney, one of today's important artists, spoke (on the videotape) about his work and explained his technique. Students then used cameras to explore Hockney's photo collage technique in their own environment. Student groups can arrange several sets of their photos differently—telling unique stories with different compositions of the same pictures. They can even add brief captions or poems to make more connections to the language arts, social studies, science, or music. Photographers know that the meanings of their pictures depend to a large extent on the words that go with them.

Note: teachers do need to preview any videos before they are used in the classroom because some parts may not be appropriate for elementary school children. Teachers can also select particular elements and transfer them from one VCR to another so that only the useful segments are present on the tape used in class.

Activity 3: Painting with Water Colors and Straws

In this activity students simply apply a little suction to a straw that is dipped in tempera paint. Working in pairs, students then gently blow the paint out onto a sheet of blank paper to create interesting abstract designs.

Activity 4: Creating Paintings with Oil-Based Paints Floating on Water

Put students into groups of three and have them put different-colored oil-based paints on a flat dish of water. Apply paper. Watch it soak up the paint and water. Pull it out and let it dry.

EXPANDING SOCIAL AND PERSONAL VISIONS OF THE ARTS

Teachers can create a space for the arts to flourish—a sense of opening—that helps free students from the predicted and the expected. Using the arts to inquire and sense openings results in what Emily Dickinson called "a slow fire lit by the imagination." As America moves through the new millennium, we need all the imagination we can get.

Advancing understanding, culture, art, creativity, and human values has everything to do with the life and quality of this nation. Nevertheless, educational decision makers often don't pay much attention to these issues. In the United States, for example, the arts are most often found on the fringes of the curriculum and instruction. This is due in part to not having a long tradition of broadly prizing artistic expression beyond the cute and the comfortable. Little is expected of citizens or leaders when it comes to knowledge about artistic forms.

The arts can open new horizons, enrich the spirit, and help educate students to expand cultural visions. An artistic perspective can color the way we see other aspects of social and educational change. When the arts are viewed as a personal luxury—and not traditionally associated with "real wage-earning" occupations—developing or maintaining a good arts education program is more difficult. This is a disappointing portrait of us, a reflection not of human strength and aesthetic vision, but of their absence. Restoring faith in the arts—and arts education—means expanding the margins to restore faith in ourselves as a nation.

Human societies have always depended on the arts to give insight into truths, however painful or unpopular they may be. In many countries today, there is wide agreement that the arts can aid children in developing creativity, becoming good citizens, and being productive workers. The basic notion is that the person and the world are poorer without the arts.

A country's richness of knowledge, enlightenment, and enduring resources for thoughtfulness also benefit from artistic endeavors. From Asia to Europe, serious arts education is one of the integrating features of the school curriculum. Such an investment in the arts is seen as an investment in the community—and vice versa. Americans are beginning to take notice.

Inventing the future of arts education means expanding the links within the arts, community, and the schools. There is a world out there that students must explore with the arts if they are to be broadly educated—to say nothing of developing self-examination, critical thinking, and problem-solving skills. All these qualities can be taught and reinforced through the arts. They can also help children integrate thinking skills by engaging in such activities as producing critiques, reflecting on aesthetic concerns, and dealing with the nature of our humanity.

Children and young adults frequently have the innate ability to do creative work in the arts. What's frequently missing are basic artistic understandings and the opportunity for expression and analysis. Experience within a discipline matters because it is hard to do something new unless some of it is automatic.

When students have the chance to express themselves, there is the excitement of producing in their own way—conveying their personal aesthetic experience through the use of figurative language (metaphors, similes, etc.) in their writing and symbolism in their painting. The challenge is to provide the necessary background and open doors so that meaningful concepts and images will emerge (Starr, 2004).

INCLUDING ART EDUCATION IN SCHOOL REFORM

In an effort to make arts education part of the national curriculum reform, a series of *Discipline Based Art Education* reports has been put forward by the Getty Foundation. These reports encourage the schools to help students go beyond crafts to art criticism, history, and aesthetics. In some of the small-scale projects, art educators, historians, philosophy professors, and local teachers gathered to collaborate in making aesthetics less mysterious for children and young adults. It was felt that even at early levels, students need to be grounded in the ability to reflect on art, study the discipline, and test out the skills involved in production.

The United States provides an example of a national effort to make sure that the arts touch every classroom. The National Endowment for the Arts (NEA) has an agreement with the U.S. Department of Education to create an "in-depth arts-in-education program" that could be part of the effort to "reinvent" American schools.

The arts are recognized as representing a body of knowledge—as well as a practical study of technique. Isolated school experiments are proving that there are a number of ways of doing this beautifully on a small scale. The question is whether the call for "world-class standards" in the arts will mean real change for a significant number of schools.

Although the connection to a rich artistic tradition is important, no response should be considered *the* "right" one. In fact, seeking the rewards of what some adults see as good creative products often makes their appearance less likely. Instead, teachers can mix modeling intellectual stimulation with the natural rapport and creative production that is such an important part of the mysterious art of good teaching.

Art criticism, history, and aesthetics contribute to production and a child's ability to draw inferences and interpret the powerful ideas. Art (like television, reading, or mathematics) makes use of certain conventions and symbol systems to express figurative meaning. In the visual arts, for example, this may include symbols in art's expression through style (the fine detail), composition (arrangement of elements), and creating the possibility for multiple meanings. "Reading" an artist's symbols is as much of a skill as reading print or video images.

Art means going beyond the transient messages that are often overvalued by the culture. In a multicultural society, it also means weaving artistic material (visual arts, movement, and music) from other cultures into the curriculum, enabling students to creatively confirm the truth and beauty of their heritage. Art is not limited to specific times or cultures: Greek art learned from Egypt. Christian art was shaped by ideas from Greece and the East. African, Chinese, Egyptian, and Mexican art have influenced modernism. A high-quality national culture can provide a unifying frame for a rich multiplicity of cultural influences (Gelineau, 2004).

Exposing children to a variety of artistic forms and materials will make it easier to locate areas of strength and weakness. All students may have a similar range of choices, but it is how these choices are made that counts. Choosing from a variety of artistic and intellectual possibilities is beneficial for building both the strength of creativity and basic skills. In addition, the arts can help to get a dialogue going between groups or disciplines that often ignore each other.

When knowledge from diverse subject matter areas is brought together through art, the result can be a new and valuable way of looking at the world.

Children can be involved in artistic interdisciplinary projects—ranging from illustrating their own books to designing movement, to poetry, to producing videos with camcorders. Process, production, and critical dimensions are all important. To understand literature, for example, children must function as critics. With art experiences, critical analysis is equally important.

The creative effects of questioning, challenging, and aesthetic reflection all contribute to creative habits of mind and set up possibilities for action. It is also important for students to see how the arts can set up possibilities for positive action and can take on our world concerns. The Art Institute of Los Angeles, for example, was asked to provide design concepts and tools to help solve problems such as creating affordable housing, attractive parks, small shopping centers, and ways to make the community more aesthetically pleasing.

CREATING POSSIBILITIES

Some Ideas for Incorporating Art Expressions across Subject Areas

What if? These are magic words. They add exciting new possibilities to our world and the world of the child. "What if I would drop a rock into this tub of water? "What if I would make a ship for the rock out of tinfoil—would the rock float instead of sink?" Since the beginning of time, people have grappled with similar types of questions. An Italian sailor asked his colleagues, "What if I sailed west across the unknown ocean?" That sailor discovered America. The sixteen-year-old German schoolboy asked himself what would happen if he sent out a beam of light and could keep up with it. That boy was Albert Einstein, and ten years later, his "what if" led him to create the theory of relativity.

In music, a frequent way of creating new possibilities is to vary a theme. Composers may start with a musical theme and then invent variations by changing it. Sometimes the melody is speeded up, sometimes slowed down, many times musicians shift keys, change notes, or add harmony. Jazz, for example, is often based on playing variations on a theme.

Music is not the only area where variations are invented. You can start with anything. For instance, teachers can vary a theme in their science, math, music, literature, history, or social science class. The way to find variations is easy, and it is much the same whether you are working with music, poetry, or mathematical equations. You rearrange the parts of what you began with, looking for new arrangements.

USING THE ARTS TO PROVIDE ACCESS TO EVENTS

The arts can provide openings to other subjects by opening the imagination to other areas of understanding. They fit naturally into the whole language (literature-based) movement in reading. Literature has always connected directly to the arts. So has social studies and the concern about understanding cultural differences. Ethnic background images must be made available in schools. But good choices are harder to come by. The typical painting of Native Americans, for example, represents a romantic vision of Indian life that obscures the damage done (to them) and the hard realities of their lives. If teachers aren't careful, they will simply add to the mound of sentimental clichés tying non-European cultures to the "cutesy" in American life.

Aesthetic creativity seems to be deeply rooted in how a child's early symbolic products convey the meaning of his or her world. Even very young children can describe, interpret, and evaluate their visual and auditory perceptions. Adult creative effort often draws on such early efforts in the arts. Creativity in any realm rarely occurs from scratch. Most often it is a combination of choices within a particular area. Prizing imaginative insight and artistic expression in children should be viewed as essential to cognitive competence and effective citizenship. There is an aesthetic world out there that youngsters must explore if they are to be truly educated in any subject.

The arts can motivate the social, civic, cognitive, personal, and aesthetic development of students. They can also provide evidence of a shared national perspective while celebrating multicultural diversity. In spite of differences, we share certain common cultural values that are separate from European, Asian, or African traditions. This multicultural perspective is built on the premise that human lives are fully real and valuable no matter how far from the engines of power and celebrity they are lived.

There has to be an open dialogue to honor the cross section of students found in schools today. This means exhibiting student artistic expression so that the students' thinking is made public. Many local papers will, for example, devote an occasional section to advertisements designed by students. What an opportunity for artistic design, connection to the mass media, and communication! So is using a camcorder to create a spin-off of thirty- or sixty-second TV commercials. Many cable TV systems are even required to run these items as part of their community access agreements.

Is the future of artistic design going to be guided by benevolent software pieces of distilled mathematics (algorithms)? It's unlikely. Binary digits (bits) will probably not overwhelm the atoms of the physical world. A better guess would be that the digital future will be a marriage with the physical world, rather than a takeover of it.

Placing the arts closer to the heart of school reform is important to civic values and the full functioning of the human mind. The arts can help convey the notion that we are all one humane world where the arts can't be separated from thinking, dreaming, and social change. There is danger in the belief that the isolated self is the center of the universe and that getting in touch with one's feelings is more important than rational discourse. When it becomes more important to focus on your own problems than on larger social issues, bad things start to happen.

The arts are particularly effective in reducing insecurity. By sharing a commitment to one another and honoring what each individual brings to the process, students gain many access points to the arts, other subjects, and the world. Solid intercultural friendships and a broad consensus that doesn't accept bigotry can reduce the display of intentional bias and inadvertent discriminatory behavior. Arts programs can help the early formation of strong multicultural relationships and make a major contribution to intergroup understanding.

THE POWER TO DEFINE, CHALLENGE, AND EXPLORE

Even the Eurocentric tradition of art has borrowed from others and the geopolitical circumstances of its time. Influences fly in every direction. The arts are both an end in themselves and a means to achieve other ends. They have the power to define us, challenge us, and help us explore the frontiers of human existence. The effect goes well beyond the art room or performance space to connect to other domains.

Herbert Reed once said that the goal of education is the creation of "artists"—people who can creatively make things with potential social impact. Good art participates in the creation of culture. Malcolm Mugge-ridge described this process as a natural café of the mind, in which we are all the clientele, a meeting place that can be raucous, at times both politi-cal assembly and place of entertainment, dance floor and theater with all kinds of rooms off it.

In one sense even science, in the context of invention, is seen as an art form because the arts sharpen the imagination, providing openings to the untried. Good teachers play a key role in preparing the public for difficult concepts, in much the same way art critics prepared the public for nonre-alistic art. To generate ideas perhaps we do need a rowdy natural café of the mind where you can find every discipline, a band, and a dance floor.

CONNECTING TO MODELS OUTSIDE SCHOOL

Fostering creativity in the arts means encouraging students to think for themselves, coming up with different solutions to problems by linking arts education to their personal experiences. Just as it is in life outside school, creativity involves innovative answers to questions that can sometimes change the very nature of the question itself.

Creating an educational renaissance will require all the community resources educators can connect with. Some schools are experimenting with residencies by area artists. Others have connected to adult models by sponsoring projects on sites (an art gallery, symphony hall, the ballet company). There can be developed in-depth thematic units that allow students to work on-site to solve real-world and complex problems, understand subject matter in depth, and make connections across disci-plines.

Getting students interested in a topic or problem and interacting with others in an environment that allows thoughtful and creative expression are objectives that few educators will disagree with. Yet how, with to-day's already cluttered curriculum, testing requirements, and red tape, does a teacher find time to unearth art topics of interdisciplinary interest? Team training can help to share the load, and community resources can free up some teacher time. But to keep reform going, we are going to have to change organizational structures and protect teachers from bu-reaucratic requirements.

Teachers can supply classroom vignettes about effective teaching: the butterfly that "hatched" from a chrysalis in their classroom, students' creative language experience stories, movement (dance), creative dramat-ics, and painting murals. Other teachers might recall the newscast of the whale trapped in the ice that spawned an array of activities: research on whales, letters to elected representatives, a bulletin board charting bird migration patterns, and an attitude survey graph. Good teachers know that to be really excited about a subject, they must really care about it.

The social forces surrounding a field of study and individual talent are important factors in generating (or inhibiting) creativity. As far as arts education is concerned, this means legitimizing its goals by becoming an active force in educational change, assuming a more aggressive role with "at-risk" students, and focusing on the potential of the arts to foster thinking skills and problem-solving abilities.

All social and educational institutions convey messages that can affect creativity and artistic development. Deep questions of value are involved in the kinds of models we set and our methods for evaluating artistic products. Art may belong to everyone, but being literate in the subject means being able to understand, critique, and create in a whole array of symbol systems.

It's best to get high-quality instructional experiences and training early on. As children gain more aesthetic understanding, teachers can think of them as participants in the artistic process. As students paint their own paintings, compose music, and collaborate in arranging their own dances, they come to experience the inner nature of how aesthetic creativity develops.

CLASSROOM ACTIVITIES THAT INVITE THOUGHTFULNESS: IDEAS FOR TEACHERS

Create Writing Partnerships

A common collaborative learning strategy is to divide the partnership into a "thinker" and a "writer." One partner reads a short concept or question out loud and says what he or she thinks the answer should be. The writer writes it down if he or she agrees. If not he or she tries to convince the "thinker" that there is a better answer. If agreement cannot be reached, he or she writes two answers and initials one.

Literature and Movement

Some poems, stories, myths, and ballads are particularly suited to interpretation through movement. Choose one or two students to read while the others respond to the reading with creative movements. Create a magical atmosphere with poetry. Use penlights in a darkened classroom or use colorful ribbons for creative movement that requires group effort and harmony. While the teacher or one of the children reads, have the other children reflect or enact the poem in movement. Each child can hold a penlight or ribbon to help create an effect.

Improvise Short Original Music Pieces

Students can improvise music pieces and variations on existing pieces, using voices or instruments (e.g., traditional, nontraditional, jazz, rock, electronic).

Working with a Partner in the Art Museum

In an art museum, students might focus on a few paintings or pieces of sculpture. Have students make up a question or two about some aspect of the art they wish to explore further—and respond to five or six questions from the list in a notebook or writing pad they take with them.

Possible Questions for Reflection

- Compare and contrast technology and art as ways for viewing the past, present, or future differently.
- How is the artwork put together?
- How are pictures, pottery, and music used to communicate?
- How did the creator of the visual art image expect the viewer to react or respond? Is the content or subject of the artwork the most important part of it? What else might the artist have wished to produce?
- How does your background affect how you view the message?
- Visuals are authored in much the way that print communication is authored. How does the author of a picture or piece of sculpture guide the viewer through such things as point of view, size, distortion, or lighting?
- What are the largest or smallest artistic designs of the work?
- What is the main idea, mood, or feeling of the work?
- When you close your eyes and think about the visual, what pictures do you see? What sounds do you hear? Does it remind you of anything—a book, a dream, TV, something from your life?
- How successful is the sculpture or artwork? What is your response to it?
- Where did the artist place important ideas?
- How do combinations or the organization of things make you feel?
- Does the artwork tell us about big ideas such as courage, freedom, or war?
- How does it fit in with the history of art?
- What does the work say about present conflicts concerning art standards, multiculturalism, and American culture?
- How did the work make you feel inside?
- Was the artistic work easy or hard to understand?
- Why do you think it was made? What would you like to change about it?

PRODUCTIVE CREATIVITY

Creativity is more than originality. There is a strong connection between creativity (including originality and novelty) and basic academic skills. The two feed on each other. Developing a unique clarity, style, and focus is as essential as any skill area. The rote drill approach of educational fundamentalists represents narrow thinking patterns that can hinder comprehension and creativity. To flesh out dry facts with substance, it is necessary to build on elements of basic skills to open up a multiplicity of images that can be creatively tapped and explored.

The traditional notion of educators is that if fluency, flexibility, and originality were systematically taught, true creativity would follow. Unfortunately, it isn't that simple. To begin with, teachers didn't know how to teach or model these concepts. Second, fluency doesn't count for much if all the ideas generated are simply novel or trivial. Even "originality," as it's understood in this context, is sometimes simple social accommodation, rather than intuitive boundary pushing or barrier breaking.

Traditionally, common school practice encouraged children to be plodders who saw the rules as conduits for action, rather than as springboards for changing realities. In the real world, we learn a lot about creativity from our failures, accidents, and the personal restructuring of our reality in the face of uncertainty. Taking risks, dealing with failure, holding the desire to be surprised, and enjoying ambiguity are all essential elements in creative behavior. All are difficult for teachers to teach and model *and* for many students to accept. However, both students and teachers profit from undergoing the fatigue of figuring things out for themselves.

The research suggests that one way to fuse creative thinking to basic skills is to provide a rich arts environment and enough structure for a student to search out interesting material (Herz, 2010). Skillful teachers then examine the quality of the thought that has gone into student productions and help with critical analysis and self-cultivation.

Some schools have proven that they can design learning experiences in the arts that are optimal for a diversity of student dispositions. They do this by assisting students in developing both disciplined basic skills and genuine creativity, thus providing multiple paths for student development.

Gaining creative observational skills seems to help students develop distinctive styles and gain familiarity with a wide range of artistic approaches.

Without the arts, students would be denied the opportunity to develop the mental skills that make art possible. Art is more than some abstract notion of beauty. Good art helps us rethink our conception of reality and alters our perspective. The creativity engendered can be a catalyst for information, change, and the enrichment of our intellectual, cultural, and civic life.

Artistic production, particularly for younger children, can play an important role as students produce in different artistic media. But even at early levels, students need to be grounded in the ability to reflect on art and to think about the thinking skills involved. Seeking the rewards of what adults see as good creative products makes their appearance less likely. No student response should be considered *the* "right" one. The mix of modeling intellectual stimulation and natural rapport is part of the mysterious art of good teaching.

Criticism, history, and aesthetics all contribute to production and a student's ability to draw inferences and interpret the powerful ideas. The arts make use of certain conventions and symbol systems to express figurative meaning. This can include symbols in the meaning's expression through style (the fine detail), composition (arrangement of elements), and the creation of the possibility for multiple meanings. "Reading" an artist's symbols is as much of a skill as reading print. This means going beyond the transient messages that may be overvalued by the culture.

The playful invention of a young child may be closer to the way an innovative scientist or an artist works than is the work of a more "sophisticated" older student. Both good artists and good scientists have a highly developed sense of wonder and skepticism. They share a world of complex options and multiple paths that require flexibility and energy to negotiate.

Neither the art nor the science world is well understood by many Americans. Even the well educated have barely enough understanding of art to act effectively on aesthetic, scientific, or political matters that they encounter in their personal, professional, or civic lives.

ESTABLISHING A COLLABORATIVE ARTS COMMUNITY

Valuing a range of contributions within a supportive and collaborative community can make the difference between a competent self-image and the devastating belief that nothing can be done "right." Recasting the teacher's role from that of an authority figure dispensing knowledge to that of a collaborative team leader (coaching mixed-ability teams) is a major ingredient of collaborative learning.

Making students active participants in deciding what and how they should learn doesn't diminish the need for informed decision makers. But without these—and other changes—in the power relationships within schools and within the schoolroom, educational reform will be stymied. This process is particularly important with some media (like video) because it often takes a small group to do much of the production.

In a collaborative setting, the teacher helps students gain confidence in their ability and the group's ability to work through problems and consequently rely less on the teacher for validating their thinking. This involves a conceptual reexamination of today's student population, the learning process, decision-making relationships, and classroom organizational structure. Challenges for the professional teacher in this new environment:

- Taking a more active role in serving students of multicultural backgrounds and "at-risk" students. In many cases, this means addressing non-Western artistic formats.
- Focusing and taking advantage of cooperative learning teams to foster students' thinking, reasoning, and problem-solving abilities.
- Making use of cooperative learning strategies, peer tutoring, and new technology to reach a range of learners and learning styles.
- Working to professionalize arts education and legitimatize the arts in the schools. This includes assessment of student knowledge, ability, and performance.
- Developing exemplary materials supportive of cooperative learning.

This development will have to be done with particular attention to the promotion of thinking skills, the needs of "at-risk" students, the needs of teacher professionalism, assessment, accountability, and the advent of new technologies.

Although children are capable of both imitation and figuring out structure on their own, they can use mechanisms for thinking and digging deeply into subject matter themselves. They also need structures for analyzing works of art, music, dance, and drama, that is, frameworks for sorting out what is real in the environment. Children have widely divergent talents and interpretations that they derive from their own perceptions and ways they filter the world.

It is difficult to consider products of the imagination apart from the system of values brought to it. Good exercises in art education involve students in altering familiar or unfamiliar images along lines they feel are promising. Students need the chance to try things out, reflect on what they have done, and try again. Most teachers know how to encourage or reorient students if they are getting nowhere.

Good teachers believe all children will learn and recognize the need for high expectations as they strive to reach every individual. Successful instructors are also able to facilitate, probe, and draw on additional information, examples, and alternative approaches for those students who were unable to connect with the information initially. This requires knowing enough about the subject to feel comfortable with it.

All our students possess the capacity to absorb knowledge—but it takes intelligent teaching to use that knowledge to reason effectively.

Curriculum development requires staff development. It is often adult models (like teachers) and family support that make the difference between a commitment to the arts or dismissing them as irrelevant.

Effective teachers strive to ensure that what's being learned is a center of interest for students. This often means walking a fine line as they engage students as active thinkers—without interfering when children are working well on their own. Creative experiences in the arts are a blend of informed adult encouragement and opportunities for creative exploration.

A flexible arts curriculum requires not only knowledge about each child but judgment about when to intervene.

A collaborative arts curriculum means:

1. *Active learning*

    Students exchange ideas when they are involved in well-organized tasks, with materials they can manipulate. Active learning is enhanced when students can collaboratively make predictions, find patterns, and explore and construct ideas, models, and stories.

2. *Interesting activities*

    Lessons should include activities that are designed to develop higher thinking skills, rather than quick right answers. Problems on diverse topics, which encourage speculation or estimation, are more likely to motivate and encourage students to work together on the lesson.

3. *Chances for student interaction*

    Students need to develop the ability to work together and to become sensitive and responsive to group members and group needs. There is a need for activities that involve all group members as well as a need to sensitize the group to include all members in active involvement.

4. *Opportunities for thinking*

    Students should be given opportunities to explore diverse ideas emphasizing concepts and relationships. Challenging tasks and opportunities for interaction with peers can lead to more advanced thinking and creative discussions.

5. *Teachers as advisers and curriculum developers*

    Textbooks and teacher's manuals need to be altered or replaced by teacher ideas, materials, and activities that arouse student interest and encourage cooperation. The teacher's role becomes that of a consultant, adviser, and learner who interacts with teaching peers.

6. *Lesson structure and accountability*

    Opportunities should be provided for group- or teacher-led summaries of important aspects of the tasks. Students need to discuss what they have learned with the teacher and other students in order to understand and explain the activities they have worked on.

Students are encouraged to take an active role in planning what they will study and how they will do it. One way to divide the class is to have students self-select into cooperative groups based on common interests in a topic. Students decide what specifically they wish to find out, divide up the work among themselves, summarize, and present their findings to the class.

There is much freer communication and greater involvement when students share in the planning and decision making and carry out *their* plan. Students achieve more through discussing, investigating, and working in mixed-ability groups than through working alone.

A broad perspective can amplify basic subject matter and help students and teachers become better cooperative thinkers and decision makers. The integration of diverse subjects has advantages sufficient to encourage the examination of what content best lends itself to this approach.

Like any concept for organizing learning, the value of interdisciplinary curriculum lies in the quality of the implementation. It always comes back to teachers and their knowledge of their discipline—the characteristics of effective instruction. Like E. B. White, who wrote that he wanted to keep the notes of his own meeting, teachers must learn to script their own lesson plans.

FOSTERING CREATIVITY WITH THE ARTS

Mass media and social and educational institutions convey messages that can affect creativity and artistic development. Deep questions of value are involved in the kinds of models we set and our methods for evaluating artistic products. An important twenty-first-century educational goal involves making sure that students are able to understand, critique, and create in a wide range of symbols, pictures, and sounds (Davis, 2008).

It seems desirable to have some basic skill training early on. The arts without imagination are sterile. But the arts without at least some technical skill and understanding abort their image. As children gain more aesthetic understanding, it makes sense to think of them as participants in the artistic process. Children can paint their own paintings, jointly compose music, and collaborate in making a video and arranging their own dances. This way they can experience the general nature and specific possibilities of aesthetic creativity.

By the middle school level, there is usually some division of labor, with specialists in core subjects. But at the primary level, teachers often have dozens of subjects to teach; in many cases they don't have arts education specialists. So if the arts are going to be influential across the curriculum—or covered at all—the regular classroom teacher has to be involved. And that teacher has to have enough artistic knowledge and skill to teach things like painting, music, drama, and the use of digital technology.

It is as important to get students to understand the arts as to worry about the end product or the performance. Yes, helping students explore the broad philosophical dimensions of the arts is at least as difficult as teaching students to actually do art. But, as with most subjects, just teaching the subskills involved in producing art won't get it done.

Techniques and bits of knowledge are most useful if they are integrated into a larger whole. With inspired teaching and hard work, students can develop artistic sensitivity and reasoning skill in ways that touch other subjects.

Distinctive modes of human intelligence can manifest themselves in surprising circumstances. The arts are natural to the way children learn. Making schools really responsible to the different ways students learn involves changing institutional structure and power relationships.

One of the goals of arts education is to make sure that all students become confident and competent with the arts. This includes making sure that every child has access to a rigorous arts curriculum in a climate of reasoned thoughtfulness and high expectations. In addition, tomorrow's instruction in the arts will be more discipline based and pay more attention to developing sophisticated consumers of the arts.

Improving education has as much to do with improving cultural quality as it does with increasing productivity. Much of what students have to do in the world outside school involves the ability to work in groups, self-regulate, plan, execute, and complete various kinds of projects.

It has been suggested that the arts can be used as a framework for inquiry across the curriculum. The basic idea is to incorporate the arts into research in a creative way that leads to rethinking and a better understanding of basic issues (Barone and Eisner, 2012).

Arts education can be an agent of social change in general and education in particular (Hetland, 2007). If visual artwork, music, dance, and drama are not found in the public schools, then the chances for thoughtfulness, self-expression, and aesthetic appreciation are bound to be diminished. On a broader plane, the arts can help counter the tendency for standardization in the school reform process.

Imaginative behavior involves breaking out of established patterns and looking at things in different ways. The possibilities the arts offer for a unique opening up of new spaces will be sorely missed if they are relegated to the margins of educational restructuring.

SUMMARY, CONCLUSION, AND LOOKING TO THE FUTURE

Whether it is in the arts or other subjects, fostering creativity in the class-room has a lot to do with encouraging students to make something original, pose significant questions, and solve problems of consequence. The basic idea is to help learners deal with different solutions to problems, build on personal experience, and think for themselves.

Innovation goes hand in hand with social environments that encourage experimentation, risk taking, diversity, and combining skills from many fields. The arts help in many ways—including making a contribution to wide-ranging intellectual curiosity and continuous learning. In addition, the arts aid the search for new ideas by enhancing the ability to make thought-provoking intellectual connections.

As an integral part of perception, expression, problem solving, thought, and action, the arts can offer all kinds of insights. At the same time, they enrich and burnish learning with wisdom. The arts open up spaces and help us see beyond what *is*. This clearing can help us reach beyond the mundane to something new. Along with making art, equal time has to be given to analysis, history, and culture. (This has sometimes been called *discipline-based arts education*.)

The arts can positively influence the understanding of many topics. Like mathematics, literature, or any other subject worth studying, they should be taught and learned for their own sake. Practical preparation for productive adulthood matters, but the educational process is hollow if we don't expose learners to new ideas that challenge and inspire.

The current efforts to enlarge the scope of arts education are partly the result of adding the arts to the national educational goals that call for American students to meet world-class standards in core academic areas. As the arts standards evolve, it is important to maintain the integrity of the individual disciplines of the visual arts, music, dance, and theater (drama).

Art is created in response to ideas, culture, and other works of art. It doesn't happen in a vacuum. It's fine for students to work together and get feedback from peers. As part of the teaching/learning process it is also important to help students understand how art forms interconnect with one another and other subjects in the curriculum.

Some have suggested that the arts can help students move beyond pop culture's assumption that the past is our only future (Reynolds, 2011). Certainly there are plenty of new things to say, compose, paint, and construct. You do not have to paint like Matisse or compose music like Stravinsky to make worthwhile art. And you do not have to be an art historian or music professor to appreciate and be inspired by the arts.

The historical record makes it clear that creativity in the arts and other fields can be fueled by the raw stuff of life, big ideas, and a well-informed imagination. The arts are more than pretty pictures or pleasing music. For example, in today's visual art world, digital technology is sometimes used to recycle found personal images into art. From odd arrangements of old mug shots to paintings that are built around public records, privacy protection is an afterthought. We now live in a social media world where it is possible to see images and sounds as they happen or as they are being created.

What about building on the arts to influence the future in a positive way? Do we have any concrete ideas—or do we even know where to look or what questions to ask? In 1910, for example, neither Picasso, Einstein, Marconi, nor anyone else who was asked what a visually intensive global communication device would look like would have predicted anything like the iPhone.

As the twenty-first century progresses, the arts are increasingly enriching technology, the environment, and other subjects. In the classroom, the arts help students integrate what they are learning—while widening and deepening their imagination. Clearly, informed encounters with the arts provide a way for students to look outside the usual frameworks and construct alternate views of what the future might look like.

SUGGESTED RESOURCES

Brown, V., and S. Pleydell. (1999). *The dramatic difference.* Portsmouth, NH: Heinemann.
Caldwell, B., and T. Vaughn. (2012). *Transforming education through the arts.* New York: Routledge.
Cooper, M., and L. Sjostrom. (2006). *Making art together: How collaborative art-making can transform kids, classrooms, and communities.* Boston: Beacon Press.
Cornett, C. (1999). *The arts as meaning makers: Integrating literature and the arts.* Upper Saddle River, NJ: Prentice Hall.
Eisner, E. (1997). *The enlightened eye.* New York: Macmillan.
Gardner, H. (1993). *Creating minds.* New York: Basic Books.
Lehrer, J. (2012). *Imagine: How creativity works.* New York: Houghton Mifflin Harcourt.
National Standards for Arts Education. (1994). *What every young American should know and be able to do in the arts.* Reston, VA. Developed by the Consortium of National Arts Education Associations.
National Standards for Education in the Arts. (1994). *The arts and education reform, goals 2000.* Washington, DC: U.S. Department of Education.

REFERENCES

Barone, T., and E. Eisner. (2012). *Arts based research.* Thousand Oaks, CA: Sage.
Davis, J. (2008). *Why our schools need the arts.* New York: Teachers College Press.
Donahue, D., and J. Stuart (Eds.). (2010). *Artful teaching: Integrating the arts for understanding across the curriculum.* New York: Teachers College Press.
———. (2005). *Reimagining schools: The selected works of Elliott Eisner.* New York: Routledge.

————. (2011). *Truth, beauty, and goodness reframed: Educating for virtues in the twenty-first century*. New York: Basic Books.

Gelineau, R. P. (2004). *Integrating the arts across the elementary school curriculum*. Belmont, CA: Wadsworth/Thompson Learning.

Herz, R. (2010). *Looking at art in the classroom: Art investigations from the Guggenheim Museum*. New York: Teachers College Press.

Hetland, L. (2007). *Studio thinking: The real benefits of visual arts education*. New York: Teachers College Press.

McGrayne, S. (2011). *The theory that would not die*. New Haven, CT: Yale University Press.

Reynolds, S. (2011). *Retromania: Pop culture's addiction to its own past*. London: Faber & Faber.

Seeling, T. (2012). *INGENIUS: A crash course on creativity*. New York: HarperOne.

Sinclair, C., N. Jeanneret, and J. O'Toole (Eds.). (2008). *Education in the arts: Teaching and learning in the contemporary curriculum*. Oxford: Oxford University Press.

Starr, P. (2004). *The creation of the media: Political origins of modern communications*. Cambridge, MA: Basic Books.

Zwiers, J., and M. Crawford. (2011). *Academic conversations: Classroom talk that fosters critical thinking and content understanding*. Portland, ME: Stenhouse.